BS"D

ח אב תשע"ח

This book is presented to

Gavriel Greeger

in recognition of his efforts in the Year 8 BMT Talmud class

in the 2017/18 academic year.

Rabbi Tarfon said: The day is short and the work is much…it is not your responsibility to finish the work but neither are you free to cease from it.

- Pirkei Avot 2:13-14

יבנה
Yavneh
College

Levine

Mr. A Levine

Talmudic Images

Shefa

מגיד
MAGGID

Adin Steinsaltz
(Even-Israel)

Talmudic Images

Maggid Books

Talmudic Images

Maggid edition, 2010

Maggid Books
An imprint of Koren Publishers Jerusalem Ltd.

POB 8531, New Milford, CT 06776-8531, USA
POB 2455, London W1A 5WY, England
& POB 4044, Jerusalem 91040, Israel

www.korenpub.com

Published in cooperation with The Shefa Foundation

ISBN 978 159264 295 3, *hardcover*

A CIP catalogue record for this title is available from the British Library

Printed and bound in the United States

This book is dedicated to my parents, whose love, support, encouragement and attention provided a solid foundation for my brother and me. Their achievements and their integrity – along with the nurturing home they created – have been a lifelong inspiration to me. So too is this book dedicated to my wife. I could not have dreamt of a more special person with whom to share the.rest of my life.

It is also dedicated to the memory of my father's parents and two brothers, all of whom perished in the Holocaust. We will never know what contributions they – or the eleven million other human beings whose lives were cut so short – may have made to our world.

Most of all, this book is dedicated to you, the reader. It is in your hands that the wisdom of Adin Steinsaltz's Insights – and the beauty and brilliance of the Talmud itself – can find some meaningful application.

I am thankful for the many blessings and opportunities which I have been given. I am particularly grateful for the experience my wife and I have had in getting to know Rabbi Steinsaltz, and for the opportunity we have had to introduce him to others. For that I must thank Toby and Itzhak Perlman, who first introduced me to the Rabbi, and the staff of the Aleph Society.

Daniel H. Adler

Contents

Editor's Note

This book describes a world very distant from us, spiritually as well as historically. We therefore appended a glossary to which the reader may refer for explanation of italicized words. In addition, we appended an annotated bibliography of all the books mentioned in this volume, and an historical chart.

In the footnotes, quotes from the Babylonian Talmud are preceded by the name of the Tractate in italics, followed by the page number. The names of all other sources are cited fully. Translations of the Babylonian Talmud quotations are based on the Soncino Talmud, except for those for which a Steinsaltz translation was available.

The foreword and chapters 1–6 were translated by Yehudit Keshet; chapter 7, by Ditsa Shabtai, who also edited the translation; and chapters 8–13, by Faigie Tropper. Thanks to Rabbi Yehonatan Eliav, Rabbi Gershon Kitsis, and Yechezkel Anis for their ongoing and indispensable assistance. Special thanks to Margy-Ruth Davis for her insightful comments and, as always, her help.

Introduction

The heroes of the Oral Torah are heroes of a special kind. Their stories are not tales of war and battles, and their chronicles are devoid of impressive events. These heroes are heroes of the spirit, whose acts of heroism lie in their thoughts and their words. The palaces and fortresses they established are invisible to the eye.

The Talmudic sages themselves declared that it is inappropriate to erect mausoleums on the graves of scholars, since their teachings are their monuments. What is more, the books created by these scholars: the Mishna and the Talmud, the *Tosefta, Midrash Halakha,* and *Midrash Aggada* are not intended, by their nature, to tell the history of individual scholars. Their main concern is with ideas and thoughts, discussions, and conversations of the sages of Israel.

Thus, not only do these texts tell us almost nothing about the heroes of the period, but even general historical events are mentioned only in passing. In addition, there is a basic tendency in the literature of the Oral Torah to leave things in a sort of "eternal present," in which the ideas are the permanent element, while the chronology of time and generations is of only secondary significance. This is not because the sages considered knowledge of the history of the nation and its scholars unimportant. Rather, this kind of information was not written or organized. Insofar as it was recorded at all, it remained in the private archives of the great yeshivot. Only very few of these texts have survived. It is therefore not surprising that only in recent times has the history of the sages of the Mishna and Talmud been collected from the material scattered throughout the literature of the Oral Torah. In spite of the great efforts invested by academics and scholars, the unknown exceeds the revealed.

Nevertheless, the literature of the Oral Torah, even in its most technical parts, is neither dry nor impersonal. The personalities of the different sages and their spiritual characters (and sometimes even private and trivial events in their lives) emerge from this apparently "legalistic" material. The special way in which this literature is edited – in the form of debates and discussions – produces figures which are alive and human, characters that we can relate to, identify with, and love. The many details found in the various sources, when put together, reveal the personalities who produced the Oral Torah, with all the multiplicity of types and the differences among them.

This slim volume does not attempt to provide a history of the sages, nor to describe their different schools of thought. It is intended to give a certain impression, a sketch of personalities not only as thinkers and scholars but also as human beings, whom we ourselves – as have others throughout the generations – can see standing before us today, alive.

Chapter one

Hillel the Elder

Hillel was surely one of the most versatile and influential figures of the Second Temple period. He was given the honorary title "The Elder" because of his dual positions as head of the Council of Elders and as the *Nasi* of the *Sanhedrin*. Born in Babylonia[1] he came to the land of Israel to study Torah. Apparently, he went back to Babylonia, later returning to the Land of Israel. Hillel's family was indirectly descended from the House of David.[2] This royal connection heightened the special status of his sons and their descendants in the eyes of the generations that followed. In a certain sense, they were regarded as the representatives of the Jewish monarchy even in times of slavery and oppression.

Hillel himself, however, came to the Land of Israel not as royalty, but as a pauper. Although he had an extremely rich brother in Babylonia (*Sotah* 21a), he did not want to take advantage of family wealth. Instead, he chose a life of poverty in the Holy Land, where he was forced to earn

1. He is referred to as "Hillel the Babylonian"; *Sukka* 20a.
2. *Ketubot* 62b; Jerusalem Talmud, *Ta'anit* 4:2. In *Kilayim* 9:3 it says explicitly that he was not descended from the male line of the House of David.

his living as a woodcutter[3] – an occupation which enabled him to work for only half a day, leaving the other half free for study. Furthermore, the *batei midrash* of those days were semiprivate institutions that charged an entrance fee, partly to exclude people who were not serious students. So from his already paltry wages, Hillel was required to deduct a considerable sum to pay the gatekeeper of the *beit midrash*.

We know that Hillel had acquired his basic learning in Babylonia where he was already regarded as a scholar. In the land of Israel he became the pupil of the two outstanding scholars of the time: Shemayah and Avtalyon. It seems that they both recognized his stature, although it is doubtful that others did. Hillel's rise to fame and greatness came suddenly, years later, and was the result of a rare occurrence in which the eve of Pesaḥ fell on Shabbat. This created a new situation, which at that time did not have a known halakhic solution; even the leading scholars of the day were unable to solve the problems arising from this special coincidence. It became clear that Hillel was the only person who had the knowledge and the ability to find the halakhic solution. In an unprecedented gesture, the heads of the *Sanhedrin*, of the Bnei Batira family, resigned, appointing Hillel in their stead (*Pesaḥim* 66a; Jerusalem Talmud, ibid., 6:1). For this reason the Bnei Batira are counted among the genuinely humble personalities in Jewish history, people who surrendered their position and status in favor of someone who seemed to them more fitting for the task.[4]

Hillel's official rise to the position of head of the *Sanhedrin* was, by then, no more than formal recognition of the fact that he was indeed the greatest and most outstanding scholar of his generation. However, this is never made explicit. We know almost nothing about Hillel before his appointment to the leadership of the *Sanhedrin*; we know equally little of the other sages of those days. It was an age in which scholars still strove to reach a unified opinion in the *beit midrash*. This is why

3. *Yoma* 35b. For his being a woodcutter, see Maimonides' commentary on *Pirkei Avot* 2:45.
4. *Bava Metzia* 85a. They are: Rabban Shimon Ben Gamliel, Bnei Batira, and Jonathan, the son of Saul. And in the Jerusalem Talmud, *Pesaḥim* 6:1, Rabbi Elazar ben Azaria in place of Rabban Shimon ben Gamliel.

the majority of halakhic decisions are anonymous and simply called: "rulings of the sages of Israel." Dissenting opinions, like the personalities of the individual scholars themselves, are set aside in favor of the majority consensus.

Yet of the little that we do know about those scholars and their contribution to halakha, it appears that Hillel himself was the founder of, or at least developed, a new method of study. He was the first to systematically organize the rules of *Midrash Halakha* and to use them in a consistent way that clarified and resolved halakhic issues. *Midrash Halakha* did exist before Hillel's time, but not in a systematic or standardized form. Hillel was the first to articulate general rules for *Midrash Halakha* which, in spite of undergoing a certain amount of redefinition over the generations, are in essence the basic rules of the *Midrash Halakha* known to us today.

The "Seven Principles" of the *Midrash Halakha* that Hillel taught the Bnei Batira (see *Tosefta Pesaḥim* 7:11) are also the basis for the Thirteen Principles of Talmudic Exposition of the scriptures, formulated later on by Rabbi Yishmael (introduction to *Sifra*).

Beyond the sphere of learning, however, Hillel's major impact is most clearly felt in the far-reaching changes he introduced in the public life of the Jewish nation. He created a special status for the *Nasi* of the *Sanhedrin,* a status enjoyed by his descendants for over four hundred years – one of the longest-lived dynasties ever known in the history of nations.

Hillel's period, which largely parallels that of King Herod, was not an easy one in terms of the role and influence of Jewish leadership. At that time, the king of Judea ceased to express the will of the Jewish people, gradually becoming a more or less tolerable foreign ruler. The High Priest, too, became a mere religious functionary. Hillel shaped a new role for the *Nasi* of the *Sanhedrin* as the national leader, patterned on the role and status of Moses – namely, that the *Nasi,* the spiritual head of the nation, served as the preeminent figure in almost every sphere of life. Like Moses, Hillel lived to the great age of 120 years (*Sifrei,* Deuteronomy 357). Two other sages reached that age: Hillel's outstanding pupil Rabban Yoḥanan ben Zakkai, and Rabbi Akiva (*Sukka* 28a) – each of whom, in his turn was, like Hillel, the central pillar of the Jewish people. It is through them that Jewish tradition was transmitted and reshaped, not only for their time, but for the generations that followed. Indeed, Hillel became such a pivotal figure that his sons and their sons after them – some of whom were great men in their own right – derived their power from the fact that they were his descendants.

Hillel was famous as a lover of humanity, and even more for his appreciation of the uniqueness of each person he encountered. He was known for his ability to address each one who approached him in a way that was most appropriate for that person. An interesting expression of this ideal is his attempt to summarize the Torah on "one leg":[5] "Do not do unto others what you would not have them do unto you." This negative formulation of the Biblical passage: "Love your neighbor as yourself" (Leviticus 19:18) expresses most aptly the notion that each of us has unique qualities, and therefore one must not judge others by the same criteria that one uses to judge oneself.

The verse "You shall open your hand to him [i.e., your poor brother] and provide him with all that he requires, all that is lacking unto him" (Deuteronomy 15:8) was interpreted by our sages to mean that one who requires it [e.g., a rich man who became poor] should be provided with "even a horse and a carriage, even a slave to run before him" (*Ketubot* 67b). It is said that Hillel took care of such an impoverished person, who had formerly been extremely wealthy, providing him with a horse and carriage and a slave to run before him. Once, when he could not find a slave to do the job, Hillel himself ran before the poor man's carriage, announcing that so and so was about to pass in the street. This story, more than demonstrating Hillel's humility, emphasizes his understanding that respect and honor are as essential for some people as food and drink are to others. Hillel, who himself was able to manage with very little, understood that others lived by different standards. He, who was so unassuming that no one could shake his composure, knew that

5. *Shabbat* 31a: "On another occasion it happened that a certain heathen came before Shammai and said to him, 'Make me a proselyte, on condition that you teach me the whole Torah while I stand on one foot.' Thereupon he (Shammai) pushed him away with the builder's cubit which was in his hand. When he went before Hillel, he (Hillel) said to him, 'What is hateful to you, do not do to your neighbor: that is the whole Torah, while the rest is the commentary thereof; go and learn it.'"

to enjoy peace of mind, that particular man needed a slave to run before him and declare that the great so-and-so was now passing in the street.

A delightful story about him in the Talmud tells:

> It once happened that two men made a bet, saying, whoever goes and makes Hillel angry shall receive four hundred *zuz* (a great sum). One said: "I will go and incense him." That day was the Sabbath eve, and Hillel was washing his head. He went, passed by the door of his house, and called out, "Is Hillel here, is Hillel here?" Thereupon he [Hillel] put on a robe and went out to him, saying, "My son, what do you need?" "I have a question to ask," said he. "Ask, my son," he prompted. He asked: "Why are the heads of the Babylonians round?" "My son, you have asked a great question," replied he: "because they have no skillful midwives." [That man] departed, waited a while, returned, and called out: "Is Hillel here, is Hillel here?" [Hillel] again put on a robe and went out to him, saying, "My son, what do you need?" "I have a question to ask," said he. "Ask, my son," he prompted. He asked: "Why are the eyes of the Palmyrenes bleared?" "My son, you have asked a great question," replied he: "because they live in sandy places." He departed, waited a while, returned, and called out: "Is Hillel here, is Hillel here?" He again put on his robe and went out to him, saying, "My son, what do you need?" "I have a question to ask," said [the man]. "Ask, my son," [Hillel] prompted. He asked: "Why are the feet of Africans wide?" "My son, you have asked a great question," said he: "because they live in watery marshes." "I have many questions to ask," said he, "but fear that you may become angry." Thereupon [Hillel] robed, sat before him and said, "Ask all the questions you have to ask." "Are you the Hillel who is called the *Nasi* of Israel?" "Yes," he replied. "If that is you," he retorted, "may there not be many like you in Israel?" "Why, my son?" [Hillel] queried. "Because I have lost four hundred *zuz* through you," complained he. "Be careful of your moods," he answered. "Hillel is worth it that you should lose four hundred *zuz* and yet another four hundred *zuz* through him, yet Hillel shall not lose his temper." (*Shabbat* 31a)

Hillel's belief in the individuality of each person is also reflected in his halakhic methodology, and to a great extent also in that of his followers, *Beit Hillel*. This is not necessarily expressed in any clearly defined halakhic concept. Rather it underlies the ability to be flexible on certain problems, to distinguish not only the general principles of truth, but also the exceptions to the rule – distortions and the changes that often happen, or individual eccentricities – and to deal with them.

Much is told of Hillel's humility and patience[6] and of the humor in his sayings and habits. Some of his great patience derived from his ability to be very realistic without being overly serious. He had the capacity to see the comic and the likable in people and in situations. The man who came to Hillel at an inconvenient time not only failed to upset him (and lost the bet), but also got a series of teasing answers to his questions. Yet, despite their sharpness, these answers are consistent with truth, and also express an interesting idea: racial diversity is the result not of essential differences, but, by and large, of circumstances and conditions. Moreover, that man did not know that Hillel could see through people. Hillel was surely aware of that fellow's intention to annoy him, and purposely caused him to lose the bet. His righteousness and humility did not stem from mere simplicity or innocence and were accompanied with clear thinking and, sometimes, humor.

The many sayings of Hillel in *Pirkei Avot* (1:12–14, 2:4–7) have become, each one in a different sphere, foundation stones of Jewish thinking. Together they express the complexity of Hillel's personality and religious viewpoint. On the one hand, there was his simple devotion to the mitzvot as reflected in the stories of Hillel in the Temple;[7]

6. *Shabbat* 30b; *Ketubot* 87b; *Beitza* 20a (and ibid., Rashi); *Shabbat* 17a (and ibid., Rashi); *Sotah* 48b; *Vayikra Raba* 1:5; and more.
7. *Sukka* 53a: "It was said of Hillel the Elder that when he used to rejoice on Simhat Beit HaShoeva [a ceremony of the Temple celebrated during the feast of Sukkot with much rejoicing], he used to recite: 'If I am here, everyone is here; but if I am not here, who is here?' He also used to say: 'To the place that I love, there My feet lead me. If you will come into My House, I will come into your house; if you will not come to My House, I will not come to your house, as it is said (Exodus 20:21): In every place where I cause My name to be mentioned, I will come unto you and bless you." (The capitalized personal pronouns in this passage refer to the Divine Presence.)

on the other, we see the breadth of his all-encompassing vision, which regarded change as part of the nature of our world. Hillel was able to see the outcome, the reward and the punishment of a given course of action. He could see where certain ambitions would lead, and therefore what checks and balances would be required. All these were part of his overall philosophy. He did not need to express them constantly and explicitly, because they were, for him, part of the fabric of reality, which was also the reality of his personal life.

Hillel's life was full of sharp transitions. He came from a noble family in Babylonia to the Land of Israel, where he first lived in poverty, eventually becoming the ruler and leader of Israel. These changes of status and location, from one world to another, formed Hillel's complex approach to the world around him. He used lofty language along with simple folk proverbs, stories drawn from life, and descriptions of everyday reality. In setting and establishing the status of Torah sages, he created a new aristocracy, but he was also the first to attempt to breach the walls of the *beit midrash,* making it more open and accessible to all. It was he who abolished tuition fees and made the study of Torah available to the poor from whom, he said, "Torah would go forth" (*Nedarim* 81a, not cited in the name of Hillel). The creation of an aristocracy based on the merit of Torah study, ecstatic devoutness combined with the ability to relate to all human beings – these were among the defining characteristics of Hillel the Elder.

Chapter two

Shammai the Elder

Shammai was known as "The Elder," not because of his age but because, like Hillel, he was a scholar and community leader. The title was equivalent to that of "Rabbi," which was not yet in use. Thus, Shammai the Elder was a leader of the community and one of the sages of that generation, as well as a member of the *Sanhedrin*.

The Mishna relates that Shammai was appointed as *Av Beit Din* in place of Menaḥem, a mysterious figure of whom we know only that he left the world of Torah study for some other sphere of activity (Mishna, *Hagiga* 2:2).

In *Pirkei Avot* (1:4–12) we read of the "pairs" who transmitted the oral tradition from generation to generation; Shammai and Hillel were the last of these pairs. Hillel was *Nasi* of the *Sanhedrin* while Shammai served as his deputy and was known as the *Av Beit Din*.

Between the *Nesi'im* and their deputies there often were ongoing disputes.[1] This seems to indicate that the *Nasi* and his deputy argued not as private individuals, but as representatives of different schools

1. Mishna, Tractate *Hagiga* 2:2 records the dispute regarding the laying of hands (*semikha*) on the sacrificial beast on festivals.

of thought, or perhaps world views, of which we are ignorant today. The obscure debates of previous generations came to a sharp head in the period of Hillel and Shammai, as two distinct schools of thought emerged, each developing an independent approach to the study of Torah and to halakha.

Hillel and Shammai lived during the Herodian period. The power of the *Sanhedrin* as the central legislative body then began to be curtailed, and private *batei midrash* multiplied, making it possible for opposing schools of thought to arise. Previously, when halakhic rulings were concentrated in one institution – the Great *Sanhedrin*, whose authority was universally accepted – disputes would not last long (see *Sanhedrin* 88b), since every dispute would eventually reach the point of unequivocal, clearly determined halakhic ruling. From the time of Hillel and Shammai onward, however, the increasing number of students and the inability to reach conclusive decisions resulted in the establishment of two major schools of thought and two countering approaches to minor and major halakhic problems.[2] These schools were known as *Beit Hillel* and *Beit Shammai* (literally, "The House of Hillel" and "The House of Shammai"). This state of affairs continued for over one hundred years and was resolved only after the destruction of the Second Temple. It then again became necessary to concentrate the Torah in one place in order to establish definitive halakhic rulings.

Although the two Houses were greatly at variance in their thinking, they were not rivals in the literal sense. As the Talmud states: "They showed love and friendship towards one another."[3] In general, these controversies were regarded as the ultimate model of "an argument for

2. *Sanhedrin* 88b: "When the disciples of Shammai and Hillel, who had insufficiently studied, increased in number, disputes multiplied in Israel, and the Torah became as two Torahs."
3. *Yevamot* 14b: "Although *Beit Shammai* and *Beit Hillel* are in disagreement on the questions of rivals, sisters [married to brothers], an old bill of divorce, a doubtfully married woman… etc., *Beit Shammai* did not, nevertheless, abstain from marrying women of the families of *Beit Hillel*, nor did *Beit Hillel* refrain from marrying those of *Beit Shammai*. This is to teach you that they showed love and friendship towards one another, thus putting into practice the Scriptural text (Zachariah 8:18), 'Truth and Peace love [each other].'"

the sake of Heaven"[4] – that is, disagreement without personal benefit. This is why the conflicts could continue for years without becoming personal rivalries; for although they did not compromise their respective positions, each side respected the other and studied the other's opinion.

The many halakhic debates between the Houses of Hillel and Shammai were based on a number of fundamental guidelines, which surely reflect the respective personalities of the sages who had founded them. Even after more than a hundred years of dispute, during which the ideas changed and developed, the personalities of Shammai and Hillel were still the formative factors of each House.

The conventional perception of the disputants – Shammai as stringent and Hillel as consistently lenient – is generally accurate to the extent that the Talmud actually lists the exceptions to the rule (*Eduyot* 84–85). However, a deeper look at the personalities of Shammai and Hillel themselves and of the styles of their respective Houses provides a more complex picture.

Of Shammai's origins we know very little. Since nothing is said to the contrary, we can assume that, like most sages of that period, he was a Judean, most probably from Jerusalem. Unlike Hillel, who came from Babylonia, or Shemaya and Avtalyon, who were converts, it seems that Shammai was born in the Land of Israel, a representative of its permanent inhabitants, rooted in the land for generations.

The little that we do know of him concerns his profession. He was apparently an architect or engineer, or at any rate, a master-builder. On several occasions he used the builder's cubit in his hand to push someone away or to hint that a certain person was not welcome (*Shabbat* 31a). Shammai's meticulousness was, to a certain extent, a professional characteristic. It was the precision of one who had to ensure that his construction would stand, that the structure measured with his yardstick would be exact and well-defined. He could not afford the luxury of "approximately" or "almost."

Shammai's approach, in halakha as in his personal life, was not necessarily one of severity but rather, as our sages defined it so well,

4. *Pirkei Avot* 5:17: "What is a dispute for the sake of Heaven? The dispute of Hillel and Shammai."

one of exactitude. When the famous non-Jew who wanted to study the whole Torah standing on one leg came to Shammai, the latter pushed him away with his builder's cubit, not as an expression of anger, but rather as a statement of principle – namely, that it is impossible to study Torah while standing on one leg. Hillel, on the other hand, did respond, saying: "Do not do unto others what you would not have them do unto you" (ibid.). In truth, this answer was not meant as a definition of the Torah, but rather as an appealing declaration aimed at encouraging that non-Jew to love the Torah. For in the final analysis, the whole Torah indeed cannot be taught on one leg. In fact, all those who attempted to compile lists of Judaism's most fundamental beliefs struggled with the same problem: the multifaceted and highly complex nature of Judaism. Shammai knew that any attempt to reduce this complexity to "one leg" must, by its very nature, be imprecise. In rejecting that non-Jew, he acted with the awareness of one who is adamant about the truth.

In a seemingly different sphere, Hillel and Shammai disagree on what turns out to be the very same principle. To the question, What does one sing as one dances before the bride? "*Beit Shammai* says: [Sing the praises of] each bride as she is; *Beit Hillel* says: [Treat every bride as if she were] a beautiful and graceful bride" (*Ketubot* 16b–17a).[5] This ostensibly marginal issue, too, reflects the viewpoint of *Beit Shammai*, not necessarily as stringent, but as insistent upon truthfulness: How can a blind or lame woman be called beautiful and graceful? Against the view of *Beit Hillel* (which, in other words, says that every bride is beautiful in the eyes of the groom), *Beit Shammai* maintains that truth is truth, with boundaries and limits that must not be disregarded under any circumstances. Truth must remain intact, even when it is painful or inconvenient to hear or implement. The strictness of *Beit Shammai* is not meant to be burdensome, but rather to preserve the limits, to clarify matters, and to maintain their theoretical purity.

As we have said, we know only a few details about Shammai the man himself. According to one source, Shammai did not want to feed

5. *Ketubot* 16b. This reflects the Jewish custom of dancing and singing in front of the bride and groom to increase the sense of rejoicing. It is customary to compliment and flatter the newlywed couple in these songs.

his young son on Yom Kippur, because he did not feel comfortable giving food to someone on that day. He therefore fed his son with only one hand, while the sages ruled that he should have fed him with both hands (*Tosefta, Yoma* 5:2). He recoiled from feeding the child because of the sanctity of the day, but he would not let the child go hungry. Thus he tried to set a limit: if a child is to be fed, it should be done in a way that differs from his feeding on a regular day. In a similar vein, there is the story of Shammai's concern for his newborn grandson: during the festival of Sukkot he removed part of the roof and built a *succah* over the bed, so that the newborn could fulfill the precept of sitting in the Sukka together with his mother (*Sukka* 28a). These stories reflect warm and close personal relationships. However, the basic assumption remains: one cannot change the law ad hominem. The rules must be absolute and uncompromising, the right thing must be done.

These alternative approaches are, in the deepest sense, what distinguishes the schools of Hillel and Shammai, as well as the personalities of the founding sages themselves. Their disputes in every area, from the recital of the Shema to issues of family purity, revolve around the same axis. *Beit Shammai* represents an essentially idealistic approach which strives to attain the utopian, no matter how uncomfortable or impractical. *Beit Shammai* regards theory as substantive in its own right, is less concerned with its practical and temporal expressions, and deals more with its perfect theoretical expression. In this sense, *Beit Shammai* sees things almost in the perspective of infinity, while *Beit Hillel* sees things from the point of view of the operative, existential reality.

One of the fiercest disputes between the two schools revolves around the edicts known in Talmud as "The Eighteen." The Mishna[6] relates that on a certain occasion, members of *Beit Shammai* outnumbered those of *Beit Hillel* and decreed eighteen edicts. These edicts, that follow a certain pattern of severity, particularly in regard to the laws of

6. Mishna, *Shabbat* 1:4: "…the halakhot stated in the upper chamber of Ḥanania ben Ḥizkiyya ben Garon when they went up to visit him. They took a count, and *Beit Shammai* outnumbered *Beit Hillel*. On that day, they enacted eighteen measures." See also Babylonian Talmud, *Shabbat* (13b–17b), and the commentary of Rav Ovadia of Bertinoro on the Mishna.

ritual purity and impurity, and that were intended to enhance the particularity of the Jewish nation, became – both because of their stringency and because of the uproar caused by that occasion[7] – decrees that could never be annulled.

Major differences between the two houses are apparent in non-halakhic disputes as well. It is said that for two and a half years, the schools of Shammai and Hillel debated whether it was better for man to have been created or whether it would have been better for man not to have been created. "*Beit Hillel* says: It is better for man to have been created than not to have been created; *Beit Shammai* says: It would have been better for man not to have been created than to have been created" (*Eruvin* 13b). The final conclusion was a sort of compromise: It would have been better for man had he not been created, but since he has been created he should examine his deeds and try to correct them.[8] Here again, the approach of *Beit Shammai* is to regard the abstract ideal as the essential, and for this reason it would have been preferable for man had he not been created. Man's life is only a shadow of a higher state of being and he must, with all the discomfort involved, live his life in accordance with the abstract ideals concomitant with that higher existence.

In another instance, *Beit Shammai* argues with *Beit Hillel* on the question of "What was created first." *Beit Shammai* says: Heaven was created first; and *Beit Hillel* says: The earth was created first (*Hagiga* 12a). This question is actually an inquiry into what is the essential. It is characteristic of *Beit Shammai* to state that Heaven was created first. Their whole approach is that earth is secondary to Heaven, a mere afterthought to the essence of creation – Heaven. They derive this from the

7. Babylonian Talmud, *Shabbat* 17a. "A sword was planted in the *beit midrash* and it was proclaimed: He who would enter, let him enter; but he who would depart, let him not depart. And on that day, Hillel sat submissive before Shammai, like one of his disciples, and it was as grievous to Israel as the day when the [golden] calf was made." See also the Jerusalem Talmud, Tractate Shabbat 1:2, from which it appears that blood may have been shed that day.
8. The compromise was that "Should it fall in his lot to perform a mitzva, the loss occasioned by its performance should be weighed against its reward; and he should not abstain from performing it because of the loss, since its reward is to be given in the next world" (Rashi on *Shabbat* 17a).

text "Heaven is my throne and the earth is my footstool" (Isaiah 66:2), asking: "Does one make a footstool [first] and afterwards make the throne?" That is to say, this world is no more than a footstool, a corridor to the reception room, a pale shadow of another reality.

The many disputes between the schools of Shammai and Hillel, like the few recorded disputes between the two sages themselves,[9] express two distinct world views. *Beit Shammai* regards reality through the prism of the ideal of the world beyond. For this reason, reality must surrender to the ideal, must be defined by clear-cut rulings, without compromise, and woe to any obstacle that gets in the way, for it is doomed to be eliminated. *Beit Hillel* begins, in a certain sense, from the ground, from reality, and theirs is a pragmatic, although not necessarily compromising approach, one which takes reality into account, and considers human problems, sensitivities, and vagaries.

The seemingly severe approach of *Beit Shammai*, then, is an expression of attraction to the ideal, to the concept of perfection, to the vision taken to its conclusion. Like Shammai the Elder himself, the architect who builds an edifice and cannot bear the thought that it will not be perfect from foundation to rooftop, the halakha of *Beit Shammai* is meant to be a perfect structure, with no deviations and deflections, a building that will never collapse, because it has been constructed according to absolute rules.

9. *Eduyot* 1:1, 1:3, and *Shabbat* 15a: "Rabbi Huna said: Shammai and Hillel disputed in three instances," etc. See also the Jerusalem Talmud, *Hagiga* 2:6, which lists also the dispute mentioned in the Mishna, *Hagiga* 2:2 op. cit.

Chapter three

Rabban Yoḥanan ben Zakkai

For many years – the final generations of the Second Temple Period and the period following its destruction – Rabban Yoḥanan ben Zakkai was one of the central personalities in the Jewish world. Rabban Yoḥanan was among the younger pupils of Hillel the Elder,[10] and in time became one of the pillars of *Beit Hillel* and its dynasty of *Nesi'im*. For a time he even held the official status of *Nasi* of Israel. He is unique in that he was the only person outside the direct descendants of Hillel to bear the title Rabban – that is, our Rabbi, the Rabbi of all Israel.

10. *Sukka* 28a: "Our Rabbis taught: Hillel the Elder had eighty disciples, thirty of whom were worthy of the Divine Spirit resting upon them as [it did upon] Moses our teacher, and thirty of whom were worthy that the sun should stand still for them as [it did for] Joshua bin Nun (Joshua 10:12), and the remaining twenty were ordinary. The greatest of them was Yonatan ben Uzziel. The smallest of them was Yoḥanan ben Zakkai." And in the Jerusalem Talmud, *Nedarim* 3:6: "It happened that Hillel fell sick and all his pupils came to visit him. Rabbi Yoḥanan ben Zakkai stood in the courtyard. He [Hillel] said to them: Where is the youngest of you, he who is father of wisdom and a father to the generations to come?"

Even when others held the position of *Nasi,* Rabban Yoḥanan ben Zakkai was considered a pivotal leader. He was one of the great Torah scholars, perhaps the greatest disseminator of Torah of his day. Renowned scholars such as Rabbi Eliezer ben Hyrkanus, Rabbi Yehoshua ben Ḥanania, and many others who constituted the leadership of the Oral Torah in later generations, were among his pupils.[11]

As a central personality over several generations, Rabban Yoḥanan saw himself responsible, to a certain degree, for establishing principles for the future course of Jewish history. This found expression in his activities following the destruction of the Second Temple, prior to the Great Revolt and during the Revolt itself.

In the relatively tranquil period which preceded the Great Revolt, Rabban Yoḥanan was the outstanding figure among the *Perushim* (Pharisees). He acted consistently – often taking extreme, rigorous measures – in order to uproot the remnants of the rule of the *Tzedukim* (Sadducees), both from the government and the *Sanhedrin* and from the Temple ritual. Rabbi Yoḥanan used to debate with the Sadducean leadership, usually in a tone of superiority, often with inordinate sharpness. A familiar phrase of his was: "Let not the whole of our Torah be only an idle conversation of yours" (*Bava Batra* 115a). In his attempts to impose the Pharisaic tradition and that of the School of Hillel as the accepted canon, Rabban Yoḥanan was not too particular about the means he chose. One of the less familiar stories about him relates that during an argument with the High Priest (apparently a *Tzeduki*-Sadducee), Rabban Yoḥanan tore off the priest's earlobe to render him permanently unfit for priestly office.[12]

11. Among them Rabbi Yossi HaKohen, Rabbi Shimon ben Netanel, Rabbi Elazar ben Arakh, Rabban Gamliel of Yavneh, Rabbi Ḥanina ben Dosa, Rabbi Nebunyah ben HaKana, Rabbi Elazar HaModa'i, and others.
12. *Tosefta, Para* 3:8: "It is told of a Sadducean High Priest who [ritually] immersed himself and when the sun went down came to burn the [red] heifer (which is against the halakha). Rabban Yoḥanan Ben Zakkai knew of this. He came to him and placed both hands upon him (thus defiling him and forcing him to immerse again), and said: 'My good High Priest, you are a fine specimen of a High Priest, go and immerse yourself once.' He went and did so, and when he came back, [Rabban Yoḥanan] injured his ear [lobe] (thus making him unfit for priesthood; see Leviticus 21). He said: 'Ben Zakkai! I will get you for this!' He retorted: 'When you can.' Three days had not passed when he (that priest) was buried."

His activities in those days were, in a sense, a continuation of Shimon ben Shettaḥ's mission to impose the Pharisaic tradition in all areas of Jewish life (see *Megillat Ta'anit* 10).

Although in most cases Rabban Yoḥanan followed Hillel's dictum: "Love peace and pursue peace,"[13]his reputation as a conciliator, all tranquility and moderation, is not altogether accurate. In his own way, Rabban Yoḥanan was an extremist who believed in enforcing the principles he considered essential.

In contrast to his extremism in the bitter fight against the Sadducees, we find that Rabban Yoḥanan was opposed to the Great Revolt from the outset. This was not due to any great affection for the yoke of the Roman Empire, but because he did not believe that the rebels could hold out for long. He surmised that the Revolt would lead to catastrophe, and early on began to act accordingly. He attempted, on the one hand, to moderate the outbursts of hostility as far as he was able, and on the other, to create alternative frameworks for Jewish life.

Rabban Yoḥanan ben Zakkai, who was not of the line of Hillel (he himself was apparently a *Kohen*),[14] regarded himself as a sort of trustee of that dynasty. This is reflected in his relationship towards Rabban Shimon ben Gamliel the first, the *Nasi* of the *Sanhedrin*.[15] Later on, Rabban Yoḥanan needed all his powers of persuasion to save the Hillelian dynasty from destruction by the Romans, who obliterated anyone antagonistic to their might.[16]

Understanding Rabban Yoḥanan's perspective on his position is essential for comprehending his character and deeds. In an interesting

13. See *Pirkei Avot* 1:2. And in *Berakhot* 17a: "It was related of Rabban Yoḥanan ben Zakkai that no man ever gave him greeting first, not even a foreigner in the street."
14. According to Maimonides, in the foreword to his commentary on the Mishna, and also Rashi on *Shabbat* 34a: "He was also a *Kohen*, as it is stated in *Tosefta, Para* 4:7: 'I have forgotten that which my hands have done' (namely, that he himself used to do these ritual acts in the Temple)."
15. Rabban Shimon, who was extremely close to Rabban Yoḥanan, was apparently on the opposing side with regard to the Revolt. Formally, he was one of the leaders of Jerusalem at the time, and is actually named as one of the Ten Martyrs.
16. *Gittin* 56b: "He [Rabban Yoḥanan] said [to Vespasian]: 'Give me Yavneh and its wise men, and the family chain of Rabban Gamliel, and physicians to cure Rabbi Zadok.'" See nn. 13, 14.

conversation with his wife, he compares himself to Rabbi Ḥanina ben Dosa, the Miracle Worker, saying: "Ḥanina is like the slave of the King, and I am like the minister of the King."[17] Rabban Yoḥananben Zakkai saw himself as a minister, not in just any government but in the government of the Almighty, King of Kings, bound to manage His major affairs. Although Rabban Yoḥanan also dealt with minutiae, as did every great man of Israel, his primary preoccupation was with the larger picture, with the essential decisions of the Supreme Authority.

In his involvement with the larger framework, Rabban Yoḥanan left plenty of latitude for others to operate. Like Hillel, he was therefore able to recognize the strengths and qualities of every individual. His loving attitude to his pupils is interesting not only for the affection in which he held them, but also for the way in which he found in each one a special quality that he himself lacked.[18] His perception of the other's worth is apparent in his efforts to save the life of Rabbi Zadok, whom he regarded as a saint, and in his struggle to preserve the Hillelian dynasty – even though at the time, no individual of that line could match his learning.

All this indicates the personality of a man disinterested in any official position for himself, who felt a great loyalty towards "the Greater Kingdom," and considered himself responsible for all that happened there. Rabban Yoḥanan ben Zakkai saw his role as shaping and guiding

17. *Berakhot* 34b: "It is also told of Rabbi Ḥanina ben Dosa that he went to study Torah with Rabban Yoḥanan ben Zakkai. The son of Rabban Yoḥanan ben Zakkai fell ill. He said to him: 'Ḥanina my son, pray for him that he may live.' He [Ḥanina] put his head between his knees and prayed for him and he lived. Said Rabban Yoḥanan ben Zakkai: 'If ben Zakkai had stuck his head between his knees for the whole day, no notice would have been taken of him.' Said his wife to him: 'Is Ḥanina greater than you are?' He replied to her: 'No; but he is like a servant before the king [who can come in to see the king at any time] and I am like a nobleman [minister] before the king [who can only see the king at fixed times.]"
18. *Pirkei Avot* 2:10–11: "Rabban Yoḥanan ben Zakkai had five pupils… He would recount their foremost qualities: Rabbi Eliezer ben Hyrkanus is a plastered cistern that loses not a drop [=retentive memory]; Rabbi Yehoshua ben Ḥanania – happy is she that gave birth to him; Rabbi Yossi HaKohen is a pious man; Rabbi Shimon ben Netanel is one who fears sin; Rabbi Elazar ben Arakh is like a spring that ever bubbles forth (=creative mind)."

major processes. He never wanted more for himself than to be a "kingmaker." Even when he was the *Nasi*, he regarded it as a merely temporary state, not to be bequeathed to his descendants.

Rabban Yoḥanan enjoyed special status during the Revolt. Despite his opposition to the Revolt, which stemmed from his appraisal that it was doomed to failure, he never severed his connections with the rebels and their associates. Those same connections indeed stood him in good stead thereafter. One of the leaders of the Revolt, mentioned only by his nickname "Ben Batiaḥ,"[19] was Rabban Yoḥanan's nephew, his sister's son. In the context of their special relationship, Rabban Yoḥanan tried to convince Ben Batiaḥ that there was no reason to pursue the war beyond a certain point. However, Ben Batiaḥ, like other contemporary political leaders, while possibly convinced of the truth of the argument, was unable to act against forces that he himself had created. Rabban Yoḥanan therefore asked to be smuggled out of Jerusalem in order to negotiate with the Romans and save what might yet be extricated from the ruins.[20]

Rabban Yoḥanan's action was not a spontaneous decision. Forty years before the destruction of Jerusalem, it was clear to him that the Temple would be destroyed,[21] and it seems that his activities over the years were part of a large, far-reaching scheme. For one who was "Minister

19. *Ekha Raba* 1:31; in *Gittin* 56a he is called "Abba Sikara."
20. *Gittin* 56a: "Abba Sikara, head of the *Biryonim* of Jerusalem [Jewish terrorists in action against the Romans and their Jewish collaborators during the Roman occupation], was the son of the sister of Rabban Yoḥanan ben Zakkai. He [Rabban Yoḥanan] sent him [a message saying]: 'Come to visit me in private.' When he came, [Rabban Yoḥanan] said to him: 'How long are you going to carry on in this way, and kill all the people by starvation?' He replied: 'What can I do? If I say a word to them, they will kill me.' He said: 'Devise some plan for me to escape [from the besieged city], perhaps I shall be able to save a little.'"
21. *Yoma* 39b: "During the forty years before the destruction of the Temple, the lot ['For the Lord,' on one of the two goats sacrificed on Yom Kippur] did not come up in the right hand, nor did the thread of scarlet become white [also on Yom Kippur, a sign that the sins of Israel are expiated], nor did the Western-most candle [in the Golden Lamp of the Temple] shine, while the doors of the Sanctuary would open by themselves, until Rabban Yoḥanan ben Zakkai rebuked them, saying: 'Sanctuary, Sanctuary, why will you be the alarmer yourself? I know that you will be destroyed.'"

of the King," the direction was clear: the King's rule must continue. The problem was no longer that of guarding the capital or the Temple, but rather the preservation and the significance of Jewish existence. Leaving the walls of the beleaguered city in order to conduct negotiations with the head of the Roman Army, Vespasian, was yet another step on a course of action most likely begun many years earlier. There are differences of opinion among scholars as to exactly when the center at Yavneh began to function. It is clear, however, that several years before the destruction, Rabban Yoḥanan had already prepared an alternative to which it might be possible to flee, a base for a "provisional government" after the official leadership would fall with the collapse of the Revolt.

Rabban Yoḥanan ben Zakkai's conversations with Vespasian (*Gittin* 56a and *Ekha Raba* 1:31) are famous both for his broad vision of Jewish survival and for his clear reading of the contemporary political map. It is told that in his meeting with Vespasian, Rabban Yoḥanan addressed him by the honorary title "Caesar."[22] Although this was considered a treasonable act, since Vespasian was not yet Caesar, Rabban Yoḥanan assumed that Vespasian was not only a candidate for high office in Rome, but that he would actually become Caesar. He negotiated with Vespasian on major matters of state, in spite of the fact that Vespasian was not yet authorized to make such decisions, because he sensed – correctly, as it eventually turned out – that this was the man with whom negotiations should be held. With his success in predicting Vespasian's future, Rabban Yoḥanan tried to mitigate the effects of the war on Jerusalem[23] and, perhaps, even to end it altogether. However, since not only Vespasian

22. *Gittin* 56a–b: "When he [Rabban Yoḥanan] reached the Romans, he said: 'Peace to you, O King, peace to you, O King!' He [Vespasian] said: 'Your life is forfeit on two accounts. One, because I am not a king, and you call me king; and again, if I am a king, why did you not come to me before now?' He replied: 'As for your saying that you are not king, in truth you are a king…' etc."
23. *Ekha Raba* 1:31: "Vespasian said to Rabban Yoḥanan ben Zakkai: 'Make a request and I will comply.' He replied: 'Leave this country alone and go.' Said Vespasian: 'Have I been appointed by the Romans so that I would leave this country and go? But still, make a request and I will comply.' Said [Rabban Yoḥanan]: 'Leave the Western Gate [of the walls of Jerusalem], from which goes the way to Lydda, free [of siege], so that whoever leaves within four hours will be saved' etc."

but also the Jerusalemites were uninterested in any kind of negotiation, destruction was, after all, inevitable.

Rabban Yoḥanan nevertheless managed to achieve some of his goals, including the ongoing rule of the dynasty of Hillel, which he regarded as the true continuation of the royal Davidic dynasty. His decision to name Rabban Gamliel of Yavneh as the leader of Israel gave additional power to the *Nesi'im* of the House of Hillel. If, until the Great Revolt, the *Nasi* was answerable to other political factors, from that time on the *Nasi* from the House of Hillel was the leader of Israel in practically all areas, religious and political alike.

After the destruction of the Temple, Rabban Yoḥanan acted on two levels. On one level, he created new frameworks within the Jewish world, to prevent total collapse in the wake of the destruction. His rulings[24] on halakhic issues in altered circumstances are only part of the great change (hard for us nowadays to properly appreciate) caused by the destruction of the Temple. The transformation involved shifting the axis – in terms of the study of halakha and of halakhic rulings – from the Temple and its ritual to other areas. On another level, Rabban Yoḥanan was one of the first to establish the principle of the commemoration of the Temple as the basis for numerous rulings. He

24. See *Rosh HaShana* 31b, which lists nine rulings, as follows: "Six [are] mentioned in this chapter (1. That the shofar should be blown on Rosh HaShana which falls on Shabbat wherever there is a *beit din*; 2. That the lulav should be taken in the provinces [all] seven days [of Sukkot*h*; 3. That new corn should be forbidden the whole of the 16th of Nisan; 4. That testimony with regard to the new moon should be received the whole day; 5. That witnesses should go only to the place of assembly; 6. and that the priests should not ascend the podium in their sandals.) and one in the previous chapter (that the witnesses should be allowed to profane the Sabbath only for [the testimony of the new moon for the months of] Nisan and Tishrei). And the following one, as it has been taught: One who becomes a proselyte at the present time must set aside a quarter for a nest of pigeons. [While the Temple stood, a new convert had to bring a sacrifice of pigeons. After the destruction, the Rabbis still insisted on his bringing them, in case the Temple should be rebuilt.] Rabban Yoḥanan took a vote on it and annulled this rule because it may lead to wrongdoing [i.e., the money might be used for secular purposes]. As to the last [ruling], there is a difference of opinion between Rav Papa and Rav Naḥman bar Yitzḥak. Rav Papa said it was [the regulation] regarding the vine of the fourth year, and Rav Naḥman bar Yitzḥak said it was one regarding the thread of scarlet [on the Day of Atonement]."

was, therefore, occupied on the one hand with creating alternatives, as interim solutions for the absence of the Temple and its ritual, and, on the other, with ensuring that Jerusalem and the Temple would remain the undiminished focal point of Jewish religious life. These simultaneous responses transferred the center of gravity not only from "Temple" to "Torah," but from a single site to many significant locations. Rabban Yoḥanan established a system in which the Temple and the Torah, the Land of Israel and the Diaspora, were interwoven.

The poignant story of Rabban Yoḥanan' s death and his last conversation with his pupils[25] expresses something of what others thought of him and what he thought about himself, right before his death. At the end of that conversation Rabban Yoḥanan said to his pupils: "Remove the utensils because of impurity[26] and prepare a throne for Ḥizkiyya, King of Judea."

In linking the deeds of these apparently disparate personalities, the visionary visit of King Ḥizkiyya at such a time represents the ultimate definition of Rabban Yoḥanan's role. Ḥizkiyya, King of Judea, seems to have taken a course antithetical to that of Rabban Yoḥanan. Faced with a similar situation – he, too, was besieged by a foreign empire – he did not surrender and would not accept peace on any terms (II Kings 18). Yet King Ḥizkiyya came to visit Rabban Yoḥanan ben Zakkai on his deathbed because in the deeper sense, both leaders acted in the same way: each one, in his own era and in his own fashion, was concerned with the continuity of Jewish existence. One chose to fight to the finish (an end which might have been tragic had there not been miraculous

25. *Berakhot* 28b: "When Rabban Yoḥanan ben Zakkai fell ill, his disciples went in to visit him. When he saw them he began to weep. His disciples said to him: 'Lamp of Israel, pillar of the right hand, mighty hammer [i.e., Great Scholar]! Wherefore do you weep?' He replied: 'If I were being taken today before a human king, who is here today and tomorrow in the grave, whose anger, if he is angry with me, does not last forever, ... even so I would weep. Now that I am being taken before the supreme King of Kings, the Holy One be blessed, who lives and endures for ever and ever, whose anger, if He is angry with me, is an everlasting anger ... Nay, more: when there are two ways before me, one leading to Paradise and the other to hell, and I do not know by which I shall be taken, shall I not weep?'"

26. According to Jewish law, a dead person causes all the utensils found under the same roof with him to become ritually impure.

deliverance); the other abandoned the besieged city and supposedly betrayed it. Yet King Ḥizkiyya and Rabban Yoḥanan ben Zakkai had identical intentions: to perpetuate the rule, not of a single family, nor of a dynasty, nor of a particular political viewpoint, but of the Almighty, over the people of Israel.

Chapter four

Rabbi Yehoshua ben Ḥanania

Rabbi Yehoshua ben Ḥanania, known in the Mishna simply as "Rabbi Yehoshua," without the patronymic, was an outstanding pupil of Rabban Yoḥanan ben Zakkai. He was also Rabban Yoḥanan's notable successor as a supporter of *Beit Hillel* – as opposed to *Beit Shammai* – in every sense.

Thanks to detailed Talmudic and MidRashic accounts of the destruction of the Temple and of the period immediately following, we know far more about Rabbi Yehoshua's life and remarkable personality than we do about other sages of the time. Rabbi Yehoshua apparently enjoyed considerable prestige during the Temple period and was already foremost among Rabban Yoḥanan's pupils. In fact, Rabbi Yehoshua and Rabbi Eliezer ben Hyrkanus were considered the two leading students of his *beit midrash*. Rabban Yoḥanan seems to have favored Rabbi Eliezer, partly for personal reasons (*Pirkei Avot* 2:8), although ultimately Rabbi Yehoshua emerged as his successor. It was Rabbi Yehoshua who perpetuated *Beit Hillel*'s methodology in its pure form, and, like his mentor

Rabban Yoḥanan, felt responsible for the continued existence and well-being of the Jewish people.

Rabbi Yehoshua ben Ḥanania was a Levite, and it is said that he managed to sing in this capacity in the Temple, before its destruction.[1] At the same time, it seems that even before the destruction, he could not make a living as a Levite. For many years he earned his living from hard physical labor as a blacksmith, or possibly even as a charcoal burner.[2] In any case, wealth always eluded him.

After Rabban Yoḥanan's death, a triumvirate headed the *beit midrash*: the *Nasi* – the assertive Rabban Gamliel of Yavneh, and at his side his brother-in-law, Rabbi Eliezer ben Hyrkanus,[3] and Rabbi Yehoshua ben Ḥanania.[4]

Rabbi Eliezer and Rabbi Yehoshua were close friends from youth, but represented two opposing views of halakha. Their many disagreements can be found throughout the Mishna. It is usually assumed that Rabbi Eliezer took a more conservative line and to a large extent followed *Beit Shammai*.[5] Rabbi Yehoshua, on the other hand, represented the Hillelian approach in its fullest fashion. Therefore, with few exceptions, the halakha was decided according to Rabbi Yehoshua and against Rabbi Eliezer.

The two men were also extremely different in personality. Rabbi Eliezer – a Levite, too – was the son of a wealthy family, while Rabbi Yehoshua was a pauper all his life. Rabbi Eliezer was tall and handsome,

1. *Arakhin* 11b: "It happened that Rabbi Yehoshua ben Ḥanania went to assist Rabbi Yoḥanan ben Gudgeda [who was also a Levite] in the fastening of the Temple doors, whereupon [the latter] said to him: 'My son, turn back, for you are of the choristers, not of the doorkeepers.'" See also *Sukka* 53a and *Nedarim* 113a.
2. *Berakhot* 28a: "He [Rabban Gamliel] said to him [to Rabbi Yehoshua]: 'From the walls of your house it is apparent that you are a charcoal burner.'" Rashi comments: "A charcoal burner, and some say a blacksmith." Charcoal burning was considered a lowly profession.
3. Rabbi Eliezer was married to Rabban Gamliel's sister, known in the Talmud as "*Ima Shalom*" (lit.: "Mother Peace") (*Bava Kama* 74b).
4. *Bava Kama* 74b. In practice, Rabbi Yehoshua served as *Av Beit Din*, although neither this position nor any other was ever formally conferred on him.
5. Jerusalem Talmud, *Shevi'it* 9:8: "Rabbi Eliezer is a *Shammuti* (the appellation for a supporter of *Beit Shammai*)."

while Rabbi Yehoshua was not. Rabbi Eliezer had tendencies to asceticism; he was an idealist who leaned towards severe rulings and extreme positions. Rabbi Yehoshua, on the other hand, was very pragmatic in his approach both to halakha and to worldly affairs.

This pragmatism, however, did not prevent problems. Perhaps because of his very tendency to downplay rivalry and avoid extremism, Rabbi Yehoshua found himself at the heart of two very stormy disputes. The first was the dispute with the *Nasi* of the *Sanhedrin*, Rabban Gamliel. Rabbi Yehoshua was not always willing to accept the authority of the *Nasi*, who tried to force a single, central authority upon all the sages. But precisely because he tried to evade open confrontation, Rabbi Yehoshua found himself in awkward positions that ultimately led to great resentment of the *Nasi* by the sages. As a result, for the first and probably the only time in history, the *Nasi* was deposed.[6] In his stead, the sages nominated not Rabbi Yehoshua, who was an interested party, but a virtually unknown scholar: Rabbi Elazar ben Azaria. It was characteristic

6. *Berakhot* 27b: "It is related that a certain disciple came before Rabbi Yehoshua and asked, Is the evening prayer compulsory or optional? He replied: It is optional. He then presented himself before Rabban Gamliel and asked him: Is the evening prayer compulsory or optional? He replied: Compulsory. But, he said, did not Rabbi Yehoshua tell me that it is optional? He said: Wait till the champions [=scholars] enter the *beit midrash*. When the scholars came in, someone rose and inquired, Is the evening prayer compulsory or optional? Rabban Gamliel replied: It is compulsory. Said Rabban Gamliel to the sages: Is there anyone who disputes this? Rabbi Yehoshua replied to him: No. He said to him: Did they not report you to me as saying that it is optional? He then went on: Yehoshua, stand up and let them testify against you! Rabbi Yehoshua stood up and said: Were I alive and he [the witness] dead, the living could contradict the dead. But now that he is alive and I am alive, how can the living contradict the living? Rabban Gamliel remained sitting and expounding and Rabbi Yehoshua remained standing, until all the people there began to shout and say to Ḥutzpit the Interpreter, Stop! And he stopped. They then said: How long is he [Rabban Gamliel] to go on insulting him [Rabbi Yehoshua]? On New Year last year he insulted him; he insulted him in the matter of the firstborn in the affair of Rabbi Zadok; now he insults him again! Come, let us depose him! Whom shall we appoint in his stead? We can hardly appoint Rabbi Yehoshua, because he is one of the parties involved. We can hardly appoint Rabbi Akiva, because perhaps Rabban Gamliel will bring a curse on him because he has no ancestral merit. Let us then appoint Rabbi Elazar ben 'Azaria...." See also: Mishna, *Rosh HaShana* 2; and *Bekhorot* 36a.

of Rabbi Yehoshua that, although he was the one offended, he was also the mediator between the sides, and restored Rabban Gamliel's status.[7]

Another more bitter and painful dispute arose with his friend Rabbi Eliezer.[8] This controversy, which revolved around a specific halakhic ruling pertaining to the laws of purity and impurity, became one of great importance. Rabbi Eliezer continued to maintain his position even in the face of opposition from most of the sages, and Rabbi Yehoshua opposed him in defense of the very fundamental principle of majority rule. The dispute grew progressively serious, until it became impossible to function with the leadership divided and unable to accept the clear decision of the majority. The sages, headed by Rabban Gamliel, therefore took an unprecedented step and excommunicated Rabbi Eliezer.

Rabbi Yehoshua, at the center of both events, followed Rabban Yoḥanan ben Zakkai. In restoring Rabban Gamliel to his position as *Nasi* of the *Sanhedrin,* he served as the protector of the Hillelian dynasty. And in the dispute with Rabbi Eliezer he acted uncompromisingly, despite their personal friendship, to maintain centralized rule by the majority.

Only three people ever bested Rabbi Yehoshua in argument: a woman and two young Jerusalem children (*Eruvin* 53b; *Derech Eretz* 6, and *Ekha Raba* 1), for indeed he was one of the most dazzling debaters in Jewish history – in internal disputes with other sages and scholars, as well as with outside opponents. Rabbi Yehoshua headed almost all the official delegations sent by the sages to Rome. His intelligence, wit, and unique sense of humor enabled him to engage in serious confron-

7. *Berakhot* 28a: "Rabbi Yehoshua sent a message to the *beit midrash* saying: Let him who is accustomed to wear the robe wear it; shall he who is not accustomed to wear the robe say to him who is accustomed to wear it, Take off your robe and I will put it on? Said Rabbi Akiva to the Rabbis: Lock the doors so that the servants of Rabban Gamliel should not come and upset the Rabbis. Said Rabbi Yehoshua: I had better get up and go to them. He came and knocked at the door. He said to them: Let the sprinkler son of a sprinkler sprinkle! (This is reference to Rabban Gamliel, who had an hereditary claim to the post of *Nasi*); shall he who is neither a sprinkler nor the son of a sprinkler say to a sprinkler son of a sprinkler, Your water is cave water and your ashes are oven ashes (and therefore cannot purify)? Said Rabbi Akiva to him: Rabbi Yehoshua, you have received your apology, have we done anything except out of regard for your honor?"
8. *Bava Metzia* 59a–b. See also Chapter 5 on Rabbi Eliezer.

tation and to win an argument, without creating personal animosity or antagonism.

Many tales are told of Rabbi Yehoshua' s visits to the Emperor in Rome. In one of the most famous ones, the Emperor's daughter tried to provoke him by asking how such splendid wisdom could be found in such an ugly vessel (*Ta'anit* 7a). Rabbi Yehoshua advised the princess to put the royal wine in silver and gold vessels instead of in plain clay jugs. She did as she was told – and the wine went sour. When the Caesar questioned Rabbi Yehoshua about his advice, he replied: "I told her what she had told me," thus demonstrating that excessive beauty can corrupt wisdom.

Many other stories throughout the Talmud and the *Midrash* reveal other aspects of Rabbi Yehoshua's personality. For example, the sages came to consult with Rabbi Yehoshua about a strange will, in which a father wrote that he would leave all his property to his son when his son became a fool. The sages found Rabbi Yehoshua playing with his children, and one of his sons riding on his back. After the game, Rabbi Yehoshua explained that that was precisely what the writer of the will had meant: that he would bequeath his property to his son when the son himself became a father and played the fool with his children (*Midrash Shoḥer Tov* [Buber Edition] 92).

These qualities enabled Rabbi Yehoshua to resolve serious and fundamental issues. Only in his day was halakha finally decided according to *Beit Hillel*, against *Beit Shammai*. The power of his personality was felt outside the Jewish community as well. His efforts to persuade, through humor or polemics, influenced the Roman authorities to moderate their stance towards the Jews, and helped the Jews to moderate their expectations from the Romans. In this sense Rabbi Yehoshua certainly postponed the outbursts that led to the Great Revolt.

The *Midrash* relates that the Jews were deeply bitter after Hadrian reneged on his promise to repair the Temple. Afraid that they would explode in open revolt, Rabbi Yehoshua addressed the people, telling the following fable: A lion devoured its prey and a bone became stuck in its throat. The lion said: whoever removes this bone will be rewarded. An Egyptian heron, with a long bill, extracted the bone. But when he requested his reward, the lion told him: It is enough that you put your head in my throat and emerged unharmed. Thus, Rabbi Yehoshua said: it is enough that we have fallen into the hands of that nation [the Romans] and come out unharmed. The people's anger abated (*Bereshit Raba* 64:8).

The sages recognized Rabbi Yehoshua's moderating influence, and as his death approached, they asked him: What will become of us now (when no one will be capable of conducting disputes and confronting the forces from without)?[9] Rabbi Yehoshua comforted them by saying that whenever the Jewish people lacks leadership of stature, the same is true of the other nations. However, it is certain that so long as he lived, his intervention changed the flow of history.

In his concern for Jewish survival, Rabbi Yehoshua fought against any deviation from internal unity. This was true in internal controversies, as with Rabbi Eliezer who remained his friend until his very last day, and in confrontations with heretical groups, such as the early Christians and others who diverged from the halakha in one way or another. One such group, known as the "Mourners of Zion," excessively grieved over the destruction of the Temple.[10] It was Rabbi Yehoshua who returned

9. *Hagiga* 5b: "When the soul of Rabbi Yehoshua ben Ḥanania was about to go to its rest, the Rabbis said to him: What will become of us at the hands of the unbelievers? He answered them: 'Counsel is perished from the Children, their wisdom is vanished' (Jeremiah 49:7) – so soon as counsel is perished from the children [of Israel], the wisdom of the peoples of the world is vanished."
10. *Bava Batra* 60b: "When the Temple was destroyed for the second time, large numbers in Israel became ascetics, binding themselves neither to eat meat nor to drink wine. Rabbi Yehoshua got into conversation with them and said to them: 'My sons, why do you not eat meat not drink wine?' They replied: 'Shall we eat meat which used to be brought as an offering on the altar, now that the altar is in abeyance? Shall we drink wine which used to be poured as libation on the altar, but now no longer?' He said to them: 'If that is so, we should not eat bread either, because the meal offerings have ceased.' They said: '[That is so, and] we can manage with fruit.' 'We should not eat fruit either,' [he said] 'Because there is no longer an offering of first-fruits.' 'Then we can manage with other fruits' [they said]. 'But' [he said] 'we should not drink water, because there is no longer any ceremony of the pouring of water [as used to be celebrated on Sukkot].' To this they could find no answer, so he said to them: 'My sons, come and listen to me. Not to mourn at all is impossible, because the blow has fallen. To mourn overmuch is also impossible, because we do not impose on the community a hardship which the majority cannot endure,'" etc.

them to normative practice, by demonstrating that immoderate mourning was unwarranted, and that one must accept reality and go along with it, one way or another.

Although Rabbi Yehoshua never compromised on his opinions, and would sometimes take rigorous and unyielding positions, he was the great peacemaker. Preserving national unity and alleviating disagreements, while remaining steadfast, was his great task. His death therefore led, almost immediately, to the outbursts that brought about the Great Revolt. There no longer was a leader of Rabbi Yehoshua's stature who could mitigate, cool passions, and put matters into perspective.

With his wisdom and modesty, his ability to foresee events and his sense of responsibility towards continued Jewish existence, Rabbi Yehoshua was able to accept the authority of people of lesser stature, and to do so with humor and without bitterness. Rabbi Yehoshua was perceptive; he could discern future leaders. It was he who ransomed Rabbi Yishmael, then still a child, from Roman captivity, because he recognized his potential greatness.[11] Rabbi Yehoshua was apparently also the first to anticipate Rabbi Akiva's eminence. Contrary to Rabbi Eliezer, who took no notice of Rabbi Akiva at first,[12] Rabbi Yehoshua

11. *Gittin* 58a: "Our Rabbis have taught: Rabbi Yehoshua ben Ḥanania once happened to go to the great city of Rome, and he was told there that there was in the prison a child with beautiful eyes and face and curly locks. He went and stood at the doorway of the prison and said, 'Who gave Jacob for a spoil and Israel to be robbed?' (Isaiah 42:24). The child answered: 'Is it not the Lord, He against whom we have sinned and in whose ways they would not walk, neither were they obedient unto his law'(ibid.). He [Rabbi Yehoshua] said: 'I feel sure that this one will be a teacher in Israel. I swear that I will not budge from here before I ransom him, whatever price may be demanded.' It is reported that he did not leave the spot before he had ransomed him at a high figure, nor did many days pass before he became a teacher in Israel. Who was he? – He was Rabbi Yishmael ben Elisha."
12. Jerusalem Talmud, *Pesaḥim* 6:3: "Rabbi Akiva studied for thirteen years with Rabbi Eliezer and he [Rabbi Eliezer] would not recognize him (i.e., his greatness). That day was the first time that he [Rabbi Akiva] dared to ask him [Rabbi Eliezer] a [difficult] question. Said Rabbi Yehoshua: 'Is not this the nation you have despised? Go out now and fight it'" (Judges 9:38). (In other words: For thirteen years you did not notice this man; now go and find a suitable answer to his question.) See also Mishna *Pesaḥim* 6; and *Sanhedrin* 68a.

promoted him throughout, until he reached full stature, almost third in the hierarchy headed by Rabbi Yehoshua and Rabbi Eliezer.

Rabbi Yehoshua became the archetype of the Jewish sage. Because of his intelligence and sharpness in argument, and the wisdom and humility that accompanied them, and thanks to his broad vision, Rabbi Yehoshua was the embodiment of all that the Jewish people regarded as wisdom.

Chapter five

Rabbi Eliezer ben Hyrkanus

Rabbi Eliezer ben Hyrkanus, known in his own lifetime as "Rabbi Eliezer the Great," was of distinguished Levite lineage and, according to tradition, a descendant of Moses (*Pesikta deRav Kahana* 40:1). Nevertheless, in his youth it was not at all clear that he would live up to his great lineage. His family, one of the wealthiest in Judea, was not particularly interested in Torah scholarship and assigned him to work on the family estate. At a fairly mature age, he expressed his desire to study Torah, but was not granted the opportunity. The turning point came in the wake of an accident. While plowing his field on his own, as was customary for landowners and members of their families in those days, the ox's leg suddenly broke. On an impulse, he decided not to return home and apologize to his father for the incident, but to leave everything and go up to Jerusalem to devote himself to serious Torah study.[1]

1. For a description of Rabbi Eliezer's first experiences see: *Pirkei deRabbi Eliezer* chapter 1, paragraph 2; *Bereshit Raba* 42; *Midrash Tanḥuma* (Buber edition) on the weekly portion of *Lekh Lekha*, 10; *Avot deRabbi Natan* 6.

In Jerusalem, Rabbi Eliezer very soon became a student of Rabban Yoḥanan ben Zakkai. He had no means of subsistence at the time. Since he was, however, very proud and filled with the desire to learn – two elements that remained the dominant characteristics of his personality – he practiced a sort of double deception: in the hostel where he lived it was assumed that he ate at the house of his teacher, while at the teacher's house it was assumed that he ate at the hostel. In the meantime, he had no food at all. This went on until Rabban Yoḥanan ben Zakkai, who had a discerning eye, discovered that his student survived by eating clods of earth; thereafter he paid close attention to him.

At a later stage, he even arranged to reconcile Rabbi Eliezer and his family. Hyrkanus, Rabbi Eliezer's father, came to Jerusalem intending to disinherit his son. Rabban Yoḥanan invited him to a festive meal with all the outstanding personalities of the time. The father, while important in his own sphere, was disconcerted in the presence of the wealthy Jerusalemites and the leading scholars. Then Rabban Yoḥanan invited his protégé, Rabbi Eliezer, to speak before the assembled dignitaries. Hyrkanus was so moved that he not only made up with his son, but actually wanted to designate him sole heir. Rabbi Eliezer was not willing to accept a larger portion than his brothers. However, now that relations within the family were mended, Rabbi Eliezer could pursue his studies in financial comfort, which he continued to enjoy throughout his life.

From that moment, Rabbi Eliezer immersed himself totally in the world of Torah and apparently was never engaged, or interested, in anything else. Rabban Yoḥanan ben Zakkai described his phenomenal memory as a "plastered cistern, which does not lose a single drop [of the water stored within it]." After listing the merits of his pupils, Rabban Yoḥanan added that if all the sages of Israel were weighted against Rabbi Eliezer, Rabbi Eliezer would outweigh them all (*Pirkei Avot* 2:11). In addition to his great regard for his remarkable disciple, Rabban Yoḥanan was also deeply attached to him. It was Rabbi Eliezer – along with his friend and halakhic opponent Rabbi Yehoshua – who smuggled Rabban Yoḥanan out of besieged Jerusalem in a coffin (*Gittin* 56a), and who supported him through all the upheavals of those troubled times.

Although he was like a "plastered cistern," and despite his unreserved loyalty to the teachings of his mentors (see *Sukka* 28a) – which was one of his defining qualities – Rabbi Eliezer was temperamentally inclined towards *Beit Shammai*. He zealously believed in the integrity of ideas and was unable to reach a compromise of any kind. Just as he studied Torah uncompromisingly and without distraction, even in hunger and need, so too was his teaching intense, unreceptive to open debate, closed to other opinions. These characteristics were the very mark of his person, as it was to be etched in the memory of future generations: a great, albeit controversial, figure.

Rabbi Eliezer was particularly diligent in his preservation of those halakhic traditions which he received from his teachers. Not only did he refrain from speculating on his teachers' methods, but he would not depart an iota from the literal form of their sayings, as he had heard them. The Talmud recounts several stories that verge on the comic, regarding Rabbi Eliezer's stubborn refusal to answer questions for which he had no clear precedent to draw from. Once, when Rabbi Eliezer was a guest in a Sukka on Shabbat (*Sukka* 27b), he was asked whether it was permitted to spread a covering over the Sukka in order to provide shade. Rabbi Eliezer had no tradition on this issue, and instead of offering his own opinion, he quoted his teachers on another subject: "There is not a tribe in Israel which did not produce a Judge." When he was asked again, he replied with yet another quotation: "There is not a tribe in Israel from which there did not come prophets, and the tribes of Judah and Benjamin appointed their kings at the behest of the prophets." On the following page (ibid., 28a) we find another similar incident; and when pressed to explain why he would not address the issue personally, but rather only relate the sayings of others, Rabbi Eliezer responded apologetically: "You have forced me to say something which I have not heard from my teachers… I have never in my life said a thing which I did not hear from my teachers."

In Rabban Yoḥanan ben Zakkai's portrayal of his students, Rabbi Eliezer is described as a "plastered cistern," as opposed to Rabbi Elazar ben Arakh, who is likened to a "spring that ever bubbles forth" (*Pirkei Avot* 2:11). Rabbi Eliezer is the great conservator, the unwavering guardian of ancient tradition, consistently, fiercely, and unrelentingly.

While Rabbi Eliezer was a supporter of *Beit Shammai*, surprisingly, his closest partnerships were with members of *Beit Hillel*. He was an eminent disciple of Rabban Yoḥanan ben Zakkai, the great leader of *Beit Hillel,* and was related to the *Nasi*'s dynasty, being married to the sister of Rabban Gamliel of Yavneh. These ties, however, did not prevent him from maintaining his opinions and his particular approach to halakha. His uncompromising stand on his principles ultimately led to the tragic event which left its deep impression on future generations.

The incident – known as "The oven of Akhnai" – began with a rather mundane halakhic question that was brought to the *beit midrash*: Can a certain type of oven become ritually impure? The discussion, which, like all others, should have ended with a practical decision, turned into an event which shook the entire generation, because Rabbi Eliezer persisted in his minority opinion, against the ruling of the majority.

For a sage to express a minority opinion was not unusual. In various controversies, sages would sometimes express majority opinions, and at other times would be in the minority. Even when the ruling went against the opinion of a particular individual, he was not required to change his mind. He was, however, obligated to acquiesce to the halakhic ruling of the majority. Rabbi Eliezer, contrary to general practice, continued to insist on his opinion and did not accept the halakhic ruling even after the majority had decided against him. His assumption that he was incapable of error was probably based on his absolute, clear perspective that left no room for surrender or compromise.

This is how the event developed:

> There is a difference of opinion regarding an oven: If someone cut an earthenware oven horizontally into ring-shaped pieces, and then reconstructed it and put sand between the pieces, afterwards spreading clay on the oven to join the pieces together, Rabbi Eliezer declares the resulting oven ritually pure – i.e., not susceptible to ritual impurity.... The sages, on the other hand, declared it to be sufficiently reconstructed to be subject to ritual impurity... such an oven was called "the oven of Akhnai." The details of the dispute were taught in the following *baraita*: On that day, Rabbi Eliezer used all the arguments in the world; but the sages did not accept his arguments. After Rabbi Eliezer saw that he was not able to persuade his colleagues with logical arguments, he

said to them: "If the halakha is in accordance with me, let this carob tree prove it." The carob tree immediately uprooted itself and moved one hundred cubits – and some say four hundred cubits – from its original place. The sages said to him: "Proof cannot be brought from a carob tree." Rabbi Eliezer then said to the sages: "If the halakha is in accordance with me, let the channel of water prove it." The channel of water immediately flowed backward, against the direction in which it usually flowed. The sages said to him: "Proof cannot be brought from a channel of water either." Rabbi Eliezer then said to the sages: "If the halakha is in accordance with me, let the walls of the *beit midrash* prove it." The walls of the *beit midrash* then leaned and were about to fall. Rabbi Yehoshua rebuked the falling walls, saying to them: "If Talmudic scholars argue with one another about the halakha, what affair is it of yours?" The walls did not fall down, out of respect for Rabbi Yehoshua, nor did they straighten, out of respect for Rabbi Eliezer, and indeed those walls still remain leaning to this day. Rabbi Eliezer then said to the sages: "If the halakha is in accordance with me, let it be proved directly from Heaven." Suddenly, a Heavenly voice went forth and said to the sages: "Why are you disputing with Rabbi Eliezer? The halakha is in accordance with him in all circumstances!" Rabbi Yehoshua rose to his feet and quoted a portion of a verse (Deuteronomy 30:12) saying: "The Torah is not in Heaven." Rabbi Yirmiya explained: Once God already gave the Torah to the Jews on Mount Sinai, we no longer pay attention to heavenly voices that attempt to intervene in matters of halakha; for You, God, already wrote in the Torah at Mount Sinai (Exodus 23:2): 'After the majority to incline.' From this we learn that halakhic disputes must be resolved by majority vote of the Rabbis. God could not contradict His own decision to allow Torah questions to be decided by free debate and majority vote." Generations later, Rabbi Natan met the Prophet Elijah, and asked him about the debate between Rabbi Eliezer and Rabbi Yehoshua. He said to him: "What did the Holy One, blessed be He, do at that time when Rabbi Yehoshua refused to heed the heavenly voice?" In reply, Elijah said to Rabbi Natan:

> "God smiled and said: 'My sons have defeated me, My sons have defeated me.'" [*Bava Metzia* 59a–b, Steinsaltz edition]

A strange and embarrassing situation resulted: Rabbi Eliezer, an outstanding sage of the generation, universally admired by contemporaries who designated him "the Great" in his lifetime, was excommunicated. Rabban Gamliel, Rabbi Eliezer's brother-in-law and the leader of the excommunicators, had no alternative but to prefer the principle of halakhic authority and halakhic determination over the individualism of Rabbi Eliezer. This was a critical juncture in terms of the halakhic conception.

This event was the beginning of a great and prolonged human tragedy. For many years – in fact, up to the day of his death – Rabbi Eliezer would not compromise his opinion. Although the excommunication did not prohibit engaging in halakhic discussions with him, it did prevent Rabbi Eliezer from entering the *beit midrash*, and visitors were obliged, by decree, to keep a distance of four cubits from him. Since his students and friends felt awkward when they were with him, there were fewer and fewer visits, and Rabbi Eliezer became more and more isolated.

At the time of his death, which was a particularly distressing scene,[2] Rabbi Eliezer said: "Woe to you, two arms of mine, that have been like two Scrolls of the Law that are wound [now, and will never be reopened]. Much Torah have I studied, and much have I taught. Much Torah have I learnt, yet I have but skimmed from the knowledge of my teachers as a dog laps from the sea ... much Torah have I taught, yet my disciples have only drawn from me as little as a paintbrush from its tube." Rabbi Eliezer felt like a Torah scroll that had never been read. He contained within himself the entire scope of Jewish tradition, but found himself apart and alone, unable to transmit his knowledge to others.

Rabbi Eliezer needed students to draw from him. Yet he felt that he had not conveyed even a fraction of all that he had to give. Even Rabbi Akiva, his beloved disciple, who was close to him in many ways and who, according to Rabbi Eliezer, was the only one capable of raising ques-

2. *Sanhedrin* 68a describes his last words and the annulment of the ban.

tions in fields that no one else even considered,[3] did not come and did not ask. The frustration of the man, who felt that he was a repository of Jewish wisdom which he could not transmit, is part of the anguish associated with the personality of Rabbi Eliezer. He is the lonely man whose principles made him powerless to influence others.

Rabbi Eliezer's seclusion is reflected in the parallel isolation of his halakhic method. In the many disputes between Rabbi Eliezer and Rabbi Yehoshua ben Ḥanania, his partner in study and opponent in debates, halakha was almost always decided against Rabbi Eliezer. Rabbi Yehoshua, along with most of his colleagues, respected Rabbi Eliezer and, in spite of everything, regarded him as the leading sage of the period. Rabbi Eliezer's isolation was therefore perceived not only as a personal mishap, but as a disaster of the generation, whose preeminent scholar had been ostracized.

Rabbi Eliezer's greatness was multifaceted and not confined to a narrow and specific sphere. He was passionate about the preservation of tradition and resolute about principles, yet his scope of interest included almost every area and subject of Torah study. He had absolute mastery over halakha, *aggada,* the exoteric, and the esoteric. When Rabbi Eliezer's colleagues and students came to visit him on his sickbed (*Sanhedrin* 101a), they praised Rabbi Eliezer – who was, after all, their contemporary – in adulatory terms usually reserved for eulogies: "You are more beneficial to Israel than the rain," "You are more beneficial to Israel than the sun." A midrash relates that Rabbi Yehoshua kissed the stone upon which Rabbi Eliezer had been seated, saying: "This stone is like Mount Sinai, and he who sat upon it like the Ark of the Covenant" (*Shir HaShirim Raba,* chapter beginning "The scent of your oils").

It is no coincidence that the tradition of Rabbi Eliezer's descent from Moses was preserved. Like Moses, Rabbi Eliezer was an all-encompassing personality who embraced the entire Torah, of all generations. Because he approached the Torah as something whole, flawless, and sublime, he believed that it ought not to be touched, altered, or

3. Ibid.: "Moreover, I have studied three hundred (or, as others state, three thousand) laws about planting cucumbers [by magic], and no man, excepting Akiva ben Yosef, ever questioned me thereon."

overly debated, since assertions and arguments only spoil and corrupt the perfect, pure tradition of the Torah itself.[4] This is the source of the great admiration for Rabbi Eliezer: the man who is virtually identified with the Torah to the point of becoming one with it.

There is a tradition that in this world, the halakha is according to Rabbi Yehoshua, but that in the world to come, the halakha will be according to Rabbi Eliezer. Rabbi Yehoshua's approach is pragmatic and humane, suited to this world. But the Torah in its perfection and purity, as it will be realized only at the end of days after the coming of the Messiah, is expressed by Rabbi Eliezer the Great.

4. Mishna, *Nega'im* 9:3: "Rabbi Yehuda ben Batira said [to Rabbi Eliezer]: 'I would submit argument on it.' The other replied: 'If you would thereby confirm the ruling of the sages well and good.'" Rabbi Ovadia of Bertinoro, the medieval commentator, adds: "If you find reason to support the ruling of the sages… – say it; [but do not say anything to the opposite effect], for I will not lay aside what I have received from my masters and listen to you."

Chapter six

Elisha ben Avuya

Elisha ben Avuya, known in Talmudic literature as "Aḥer" (literally, "The Other") was in many respects the tragedy of the Mishnaic sages. Among the most important sages of his day, an influential personality deeply involved in the Jewish world and recognized for his independent scholarship, Elisha ben Avuya crossed the bounds and betrayed the Jewish community in more than one sense. The defection of such an individual from the innermost core of the Jewish people left a deep scar within Jewish tradition.

How can we begin to understand this personality? How can we understand what befell this great man who ceased to be a Jewish leader? These questions vexed his contemporaries and close acquaintances and continued to occupy the thinking of succeeding generations long after his death.

From the story of his birth, as retold by Elisha himself, it is clear that from the outset his personality was not of one piece.[1] Elisha was

1. Jerusalem Talmud, *Hagiga*, 2:1: "And thus it is told [by Elisha himself]: My father Avuya was one of the richest men of Jerusalem. When he came to circumcise me he invited all the rich men of Jerusalem and seated them in one room, and Rabbi

born in Jerusalem and raised in a family that was, at least by the standards of the time, partially assimilated. He described how his circumcision was celebrated: there was feasting and merriment, including dancing alien to Jewish culture, as well as an assembly of guests totally disinterested in the religious significance of the celebration. Because of the Jewish origins of the occasion, some of the sages were invited, and while the company caroused, they sat in another room and studied Torah. This apparently left such a strong impression on Avuya, the father, that he changed his plan for his son's way of life: rather than commit him to the family business, he dedicated Elisha to the study of Torah. In any event, it is clear that Elisha ben Avuya's environment did not draw solely from Jewish culture.

Elisha's interest in Greek culture, as described in the Talmud[2] was part of the dual education that he received. On the one hand, he was a scholar, studying Torah in the *beit midrash*, and on the other, he was a student of classical Greek culture. It seems that at no point was he able to completely renounce either Judaism or Greek erudition. He did, however, dedicate a substantial portion of his life to the world of Torah, which occupied most of his interest. He eventually became a

Eliezer and Rabbi Yehoshua in another. Out of their eating and drinking, they [the rich ones] began clapping hands and dancing. Rabbi Eliezer said to Rabbi Yehoshua: 'They are doing as they do, let us do as we do.' So they delved into the Torah; from the Torah they went on to study the Prophets, and from there to study the Writings (the section of the tradition that includes Psalms, Ecclesiastes, Proverbs, Job, the Book of Chronicles, the five Scrolls, and the books of Daniel, Ezra, and Nehemiah). And fire came down from heaven and surrounded them. Said Avuya: 'Gentlemen, have you come to burn my house upon me?' They replied: 'Heaven forbid! We were roaming within the words of the Torah; from there we went to the Prophets and thereafter to the Writings, and what we studied was as joyous and gladdening as when it was received on Mount Sinai, and they were on fire, just as they were at Sinai. For the beginning [of the giving the Torah] on Sinai was by fire [as it says, Deuteronomy 4:11]: "And the mountain burned with fire unto the heart of heaven." Said Father Avuya: 'Gentlemen, if this is the power of Torah, if this boy lives, I will dedicate him to the Torah.' Since his intention was not for the sake of heaven (i.e., pure or altruistic) it was not carried out in this man (Elisha)."

2. *Hagiga* 15b: "Who is Aḥer? Greek song did not cease from his mouth. It is told of Aḥer that when he used to rise [to go from] the *beit midrash*, many heretical books used to fall from his lap."

leading scholar and a sharp halakhist who was involved in other areas of Jewish life as well.

Elisha's breaking point is described in the Talmud as a double crisis: internal and external collapse, a combination which led him to desert the Jewish world. His internal crisis was one of faith. He was one of the four who "entered the Orchard,"[3] whose mystical experiences and teachings became part of Jewish tradition. However, only the greatest and most mature of the four, Rabbi Akiva – who apparently served as their guide – entered and left the Orchard intact. Two of the others collapsed, physically or mentally, while Elisha suffered a spiritual breakdown. Elisha came to accept, in some form, the fundamental tenets of Greek Gnosis and of the assimilated Jews who were associated with it. These theories, flourishing in the Near East as part of the mystical culture of the area, perceived the world as subject to two authorities: the Good, which was mostly passive, and another, lower authority, connected with this world, with the powers that rule it, and with evil.[4]

Elisha's inner crisis was exacerbated by the external crises of the era: the destruction of the Temple, the failure of the Great Revolt, the ensuing national and political collapse of the Jewish people, and the frequent edicts that forbade Torah study and observance of the commandments. The Talmud relates (*Kiddushin* 39b) that one of the factors

3. *Hagiga* 14b describes, in rather veiled terms, a powerful mystical experience that was shared by the four sages: "Our Rabbis taught: Four men entered the 'Orchard,' namely, ben Azzai, ben Zoma, Aḥer, and Rabbi Akiva. Rabbi Akiva said to them: 'When you arrive at the stones of pure marble, say not, Water, water, for it is said: "He that speaks falsehood shall not be established before mine eyes"' (Psalms 101:7). Ben Azzai cast a look and died. Of him Scripture says: 'Precious in the sight of the Lord is the death of His saints' (Psalms 116:15). Ben Zoma looked and became demented. Of him Scripture says: 'Have you found honey? Eat so much as is sufficient for you, lest you be filled therewith, and vomit it' (Proverbs 25:16). Aḥer mutilated the shoots. Rabbi Akiva departed unhurt."
4. *Hagiga* 15a: "Aḥer mutilated the shoots. Of him Scripture says: 'Do not allow your mouth to bring your flesh into guilt' (Ecclesiastes 5:5). What does it refer to? He saw that permission was granted to Metatron (one of the highest Angels) to sit and write down the merits of Israel. Said he: 'It is taught as a tradition that in Heaven there is no sitting (namely: no effort and no rest) and no emulation (rivalry) and no back (because angels have faces in all directions) and no weariness (or: no injunction). Perhaps – God forfend! – there are two authorities.'"

that pushed Elisha out of the fold was the spectacle of a pig dragging the tongue of Ḥutzpit the Interpreter.[5] brutally murdered by the Romans. This trauma – the sight of human beings, particularly fellow Jews, broken by the might of Rome – ran parallel to Elisha's crisis of faith. It tipped the scales in favor of a perception of the world as ruled by evil triumphant. It was ostensibly proof that even if a Supreme Power existed, it was too distant to interfere in man's affairs. Elisha, with all the hesitations and divisions in his soul, took the step of opting for the force which rules this world de facto.

For a certain period thereafter, Elisha fully identified with the outside world. At that time, racism did not exist. The distinction between Jew and non-Jew was primarily cultural, and Elisha was therefore able, at least temporarily, to move completely into that other world. He worked against the Jewish community and the sages,[6] even collaborating with the Roman authorities.[7] And he gave free rein to all his material desires: women, money, and other temptations. The Talmud (*Hagiga* 15a) relates that a certain prostitute, solicited by Elisha, asked him: "Are you not

5. The Interpreter was a person who stood next to the sage who was teaching Torah, and would explain and sometimes also translate into the local Aramaic dialect the sayings of that sage. To be able to do so, the Interpreter had to be greatly learned.
6. Jerusalem Talmud, *Hagiga* 2:1: "Aḥer mutilated the shoots. Who is Aḥer? It is Elisha ben Avuya who killed the outgrowths of Torah. It is told, that whenever he would see a scholar who was successful in Torah learning, he would kill him. Furthermore, when he would enter into the *beit midrash* and would see children sitting in front of their teacher [and studying the Torah], he would say to them 'What are you sitting here for? This one's trade is a builder, that one should be a carpenter, this one – a hunter, that one – a tailor.' Once the children would hear him, they would leave their teacher and go."
7. Ibid.: "At the time of anti-religious decrees [against the Jews], they [the Romans] would give Jews heavy loads [to carry on the Sabbath]. They [the Jews] tried to circumvent this decree by doing the work of one person by two people [and thus not to violate the Sabbath]. So he [Elisha] told the Romans: 'Put the load on them individually,' and they did. They [the Jews] then devised another way of circumventing the decree by unloading the burden in the Carmelit [an area which was neither public nor private domain, and then loading it again and carrying it further, and thus not violate the Sabbath]. So he [Elisha] told the Romans: 'Give them fragile utensils to carry [so that they will not be able to load and unload them],' and the Romans did so."

Elisha?" After he convinced her that he no longer behaved as a Jewish scholar, she said: "It is another Aḥer." The name stuck. He is no longer Elisha, he is no longer the man he was; he is another.

In spite of all the explanations offered for his conduct, the character of Elisha ben Avuya continued to perplex the sages deeply: How could a man who had imbibed so much Torah veer off on a path so strange and alien?

The problematic of Elisha's personality lay not only in his deviation, but in the fact that he himself was apparently miserable with his choice. His student Rabbi Meir understood this; thus he was the only scholar who did not shun Elisha. He repeatedly pleaded with Elisha to repent, because Elisha seemed neither content nor secure in the new life he had chosen. Elisha had been miserable in the world of Torah study, because he had felt that evil triumphed in this world. But in the other alien world into which he had sunk, he was not at peace either. Again and again he fraternized with Jews, over and over he became involved in Jewish affairs (ibid., 15a–b) – which, after all, constituted most of his spiritual life. He remained a great Torah scholar, capable of teaching, and Rabbi Meir, walking alongside Elisha, who was astride his horse on Shabbat,[8] could still learn Torah in many varied areas from him.

Although at first Elisha attempted to destroy the Jewish world, later on he considered himself a failure. Rabbi Akiva had been killed, the Great Revolt against Rome had failed; nonetheless, Elisha ben Avuya did not feel, then, that the Evil One was winning. Outwardly, he would attack Rabbi Meir, who was among the youngest of Rabbi Akiva's disciples: "Rabbi Akiva your teacher did not say this, Rabbi Akiva your teacher did not say that" (*Hagiga* 15a; Jerusalem Talmud, *Hagiga* 2:1). But inwardly he was preoccupied with his tragic inability to repent. Elisha ben Avuya had been too profoundly entrenched in the Jewish world for his return to be a simple matter, and at the same time he had immersed himself too deeply in that other world to be able to extricate himself.

Initially, Elisha not only destroyed himself; he also tried to influence others to desert Judaism for what, at the time, seemed to be the pervasive culture of a new world. Later on, he regarded himself as not

8. It is forbidden to ride a beast of burden on the Sabbath.

merely a private sinner, but as a wrongdoer who had led others to transgress and was, therefore, unworthy of pardon.[9] He felt that even if the way of repentance is open for the rest of the world, for one who knew as much as he did, and yet sinned as much as he did, there was no way back.

Elisha ben Avuya died alone without a single student to carry on his teaching. He disappeared from the stage, leaving the anguish and the riddle of his life for future generations. He did, however, have descendants. It is told that his daughters came to Rabbi Yehuda HaNasi ("Rebbi") to receive charity. Rebbi deliberated over whether to receive or rebuff them; finally he burst into tears and decreed that they receive support from public funds, thus effectively reinstating them in the Jewish community.[10] Rabbi Yaakov, Elisha's grandson, a sage of the Mishnaic period, was quite different from Elisha. A clear thinker, he perceived a perfect, spiritual, and pure world, and was not tormented by the problems of this life.[11]

9. *Hagiga* 15a–b: "Once Aḥer was riding on a horse on the Sabbath, and Rabbi Meir was walking behind him to learn Torah at his mouth. Said [Aḥer] to him: 'Meir, turn back, for I have already measured by the paces of my horse that thus far extends the Shabbat boundaries.' He replied: 'You, too, go back!' [Aḥer] answered: 'Have I not already told you that I have already heard from behind the Veil (Jeremiah 3:14, 22): Return you backsliding children – except Aḥer.'"
10. Jerusalem Talmud, *Hagiga* 2:1: "Some time later his daughters came to receive charity from Rebbi. He decreed: 'He shall not receive grace nor shall there be pity for his orphans' (Psalms 109:12). They said: 'Rebbi, do not look on his deeds, look on his (Torah) learning.' At that moment he broke into weeping and decreed that they should receive support."
11. *Kiddushin* 39b: "Rava said: This is according to Rabbi Yaakov, who said: There is no reward for [keeping] the mitzvot (precepts) in this world. For it is taught: Rabbi Yaakov said: There is not a single mitzva in the Torah whose reward is [stated] at its side which is not dependent on the resurrection of the dead. [Thus], in connection with honoring parents, it is written, 'That your days may be prolonged and that it may go well with you' (Deuteronomy 5:16). In reference to the dismissal of the nest (ibid., 22:6–7) it is written, 'that it may be well with you, and that you may prolong your days.' Now, if one's father said to him, 'Ascend to the loft and bring me young birds,' and he ascends to the loft, dismisses the mother-bird and takes the young, and on his return falls and is killed – where is this man's happiness, and where is this man's prolonging of days? But 'in order that it may be well with you' means on the day that is wholly good; and 'in order that your days may be long' [means] on the day that is wholly long (i.e., in the world to come)." And in the Jerusalem

Elisha did leave behind his Torah teachings. The question of how to relate to them was a basic problem that engaged scholars for generations. Ultimately, they adopted the position expressed by Elisha's daughter to Rebbi: "Remember his teachings, not his deeds" (Jerusalem Talmud, *Hagiga* 2:1). Thus in *Pirkei Avot* (4:20) we find reference to Elisha's statements, and in *Avot deRabbi Natan* an entire chapter (chapter 24) is devoted to his wisdom and ethical sayings.

In death, too, as in life, Elisha ben Avuya was tom between two worlds. He could not be condemned to Hell because of his stature as a scholar; nor could he enter the Garden of Eden because he was so great a sinner. The Talmud relates how his disciple, Rabbi Meir, begged that he be condemned to all the punishments of Hell that he deserved, so that at the end he might be granted purification (of the soul) (*Hagiga* 15b). Rabbi Meir said: "When will I die and the smoke arise from his tomb (as an indication that he was indeed being judged in Hell)?" When Rabbi Meir died, smoke did rise from Elisha's tomb. But this was not the end, for the smoke continued to rise, indicating that he had not yet emerged from Hell, since such a deep betrayal could not be expiated. That smoke continued to disturb the peace of the living until, several generations later, Rabbi Yoḥanan said: "Is it heroism to burn one's teacher? There was one (Aḥer)[12] among us (the sages) and he went astray. Can we not save him?" Rabbi Yoḥanan added: "When will I die and extinguish the smoke from his tomb (to show that he has been taken out of Hell and brought to life in the world to come)?" And indeed, when Rabbi Yoḥanan died, the smoke ceased to rise from Aḥer's tomb (*Hagiga* 15b).

Another, quite poetic, description is found in the Jerusalem Talmud (*Hagiga* 2:1). Told that Elisha's grave was on fire, Rabbi Meir went to the burning tomb, spread his tallit upon it and recited the verses that

Talmud, *Hagiga* 2:1, we read: "The following day [Aḥer] saw a man climb to the top of a palm tree and take the young from the nest and send the mother away; upon his descent, a snake bit him and he died. He [Aḥer] said. 'It is written: "You shall send the mother...that it may go well with you and that your days may be prolonged." Where is the well-being of this one and where is his long life?' And he did not know that Rabbi Yaakov would interpret it [differently]."

12. There is a play on words here: "one" in Hebrew is *Eḥad* (אחד), a word which in print looks almost exactly like Aḥer (אחר).

Bo'az had said to Ruth (Ruth 3:13): "Remain this night, and in the morning, if he will redeem you, it is good. But if he is not willing to redeem you, then as the Lord lives, I will do so. Lie here until the morning." Rabbi Meir interpreted the verses thus: "If He redeems you, good – this is God who is called 'good.' If He will redeem you by the power of judgment and justice – it is good. If not, 'I will do so, as the Lord lives, lie till the morning,' that is, the time of redemption."

Elisha's statement in *Pirkei Avot* – "To what may we liken one who studies Torah as a child? To ink written on a clean page; and to what may we liken one who studies Torah as an old man? To ink written on an erased page" – is characteristic of his personality. Originality was fundamental to his worldview: everything he learned was like new ink inscribed on a fresh sheet. The material appearing in his name in *Avot deRabbi Natan* is an expansion of this same idea: the importance of the Torah being studied and internalized in a new and fresh way.

This notion partially explains the tendency of Elisha's early years to seek out the original and the new, as well as his subsequent reluctance, after having expunged what he knew, to write again on an already used sheet. He felt that he could not rewrite the things that he knew, because he no longer possessed the primal freshness of one who is expressing new things and taking part in innovation. For him, that which was broken could never be completely restored to its original state.

Thus Elisha ben Avuya could not repent; he was not capable of writing on erased paper. But his same knowledge, even if he did not record it himself, was transcribed, perhaps intentionally, in his name. Elisha asked Rabbi Meir to interpret the verse: "Gold and glass cannot equal it" (Job 28:17). Rabbi Meir replied: "These are the words of the Torah, which are hard to acquire like vessels of fine gold, but are easily destroyed like vessels of glass." And Elisha characteristically replied (*Hagiga* 15a): "Rabbi Akiva, your master, did not explain it thus, but [as follows]: Just as vessels of gold and vessels of glass, though they be broken, have a remedy, even so a scholar, though he has sinned, has a remedy." For vessels of gold and of glass have one thing in common: when they break, they can be recast into forms that would be just as gorgeous as the original ones.

Chapter seven

Rabbi Yehuda HaNasi ("Rebbi")

Rabbi Yehuda HaNasi was known affectionately both to his students and to subsequent generations as "Rebbi." The Talmud states: "From Moses to Rebbi, we do not find another who was supreme both in Torah and in worldly affairs" (*Gittin* 59a). Other than Moses and Rebbi, no single individual exercised such wide political powers while serving as the most important scholarly and spiritual figure of his generation. Usually, political and spiritual leadership were divided between two different people, with possible conflicting interests. In the very few cases in which the domains were consolidated, the leader overshadowed everyone else in his generation.

Rabbi Yehuda HaNasi lived in the generation after the Great Revolt and the harsh Roman decrees that followed. The revolt and the "edicts of persecution," as they are referred to in the Talmud, left Judea completely desolate; a long period of recovery was required to reconstruct Jewish settlement and Jewish culture in another region. In fact, it was not until Rebbi's time that the Jewish population of the Galilee became strong enough to produce Torah scholars once more.

The state of Jewish settlement and Rebbi's own status improved greatly, thanks to his excellent relations with the Roman authorities. The Talmud contains many homiletic tales[1] of the complex relationship between Rebbi and the Caesar, known in Talmudic literature as Antoninus.[2] Antoninus not only maintained a close personal friendship with Rebbi; it seems that he appreciated Rebbi's spiritual role, and that he himself sought some connection to Jewish values.[3] This special relationship between the *Nasi* of the *Sanhedrin* and the Roman Caesar generated a period of tranquillity. In addition, the status of *Nasi*, which had been greatly weakened within and without the Jewish community in previous generations, was now strengthened in a way never again to be matched. Because of his great Torah learning, his wisdom, and his unique political status, Rebbi enjoyed unparalleled power.

Rebbi's special stature stemmed both from historic circumstances and from his own personality. In his own lifetime he was already accorded the title "our holy Rabbi" (*Shabbat* 118b, *Sanhedrin* 98b). Despite his great wealth[4] and the external trappings of splendor and authority, he himself lived a life of modesty and asceticism. His fasts and the physical agony he suffered for many years[5] stood in marked contrast to the bounty prevalent on his table and at his court. The Talmud relates that "at the time of his passing, [Rebbi] raised his ten fingers towards Heaven and said: 'Sovereign of the Universe, You know that I

1. *Sanhedrin* 91a–b; *Avoda Zara* 10a–b, and *Tosafot*, ibid.; Jerusalem Talmud: *Sanhedrin* 10:5, *Megilla* 1:11, and *Shevi'it* 6:1; *Midrash Tanḥuma*, "*Miketz*" 9; *Bereshit Raba* 11:4; 84:2; 75:5.
2. There are different opinions as to the identity of "Antoninus"; some say it was Marcus Aurelius, while others claim it was one of his heirs.
3. See *Avoda Zara* 10b; Jerusalem Talmud, *Megilla* 1:11. According to one opinion, he even converted to Judaism and had himself circumcised.
4. *Bava Metzia* 85b, Steinsaltz edition: "The stable master in Rebbi's house was wealthier than King Shapur of Persia – because Rebbi owned so much cattle, that his stable manager became exceedingly rich by selling their manure." See also *Berakhot* 27b, 43a; *Shabbat* 52a, 121b, and 122a; and elsewhere.
5. *Bava Metzia* 85a, Steinsaltz edition: "Rebbi concluded: Suffering is precious. So he willingly accepted thirteen years of suffering, six years of contending with kidney stones and seven years with scurvy. And some say the reverse, that he accepted seven years of kidney stones, and six years of scurvy."

have labored in the study of the Torah with my ten fingers, and that I did not enjoy [any worldly] benefits even with my little finger'" (*Ketubot* 104a). These characteristics, which were publicly known, added a dimension of esteem to his personality. His contemporaries, even his seniors, accepted his authority not only because of his position, but also in recognition of his unique character. As one of his pupils, Rav, said: "If he [namely, the Messiah] is of the living, it would be our holy Master" (*Sanhedrin* 98b). Indeed, Rabbi Yehuda HaNasi was called "Rebbi," without the addition of his name, for good reason: He was the rabbi, not of a particular student or sage, but of an entire generation, as well as a key figure in Jewish history. His historic importance resulted in particular from his monumental undertaking: the compilation of the Mishna.

The magnitude of Rebbi's work in compiling the Mishna can only be understood against the background of Jewish tradition in the preceding generations. For hundreds and thousands of years, the Oral Torah (as the name implies) had consisted of verbal transmission of the tradition from master to student, with nothing committed to writing. The tradition passed from one *beit midrash* to another, which from generation to generation changed their character and methods of study. One element, however, remained stable throughout: the tradition was oral, not written. It is true that in earlier times, and even during the Temple period, Torah scholars would make mnemonic notes for themselves, but these were no more than shorthand comments on unusual events or decisions which the writers saw fit to record for posterity. As a rule, the Oral Torah was not written down. These scrolls, known as "hidden scrolls" and not meant for public use, were neither studied nor used for teaching, and were preserved only as the personal memoranda of individual sages.

Moreover, there was a halakhic ruling to the effect that "the words which are written, you are not at liberty to say by heart, and the words transmitted orally, you are not at liberty to commit to writing" (*Gittin* 60b). One reason given for this was that an oral doctrine enables maximum flexibility in transmission and interpretation, whereas a written text is bound to reach, at a certain stage, a point of ossification beyond which it cannot be developed. Exposition of a written text becomes by nature supplemental, while the text itself is no longer renewed and invigorated.

Thus, alongside the written Torah there coexisted a more flexible tradition, which conveyed a practical understanding of the Torah's basic terms and concepts and, above all, explained the actual practice of its commandments. All this had been transmitted in an ancient chain of tradition stretching from Moses through the whole list of sages detailed in *Pirkei Avot* (chapters 1–2) until Rebbi's generation. This heritage was zealously preserved as an oral tradition, not to be recorded, not to be petrified.

Despite these and many other considerations, Rebbi decided that the time had come to change the method of preserving the Oral Torah by establishing hard and fast rules for guiding its interpretation and formulating it in a specific, clearly defined way that would meet the needs of the time. Rebbi apparently felt that he had been granted an exceptional historic opportunity. The situation in which a single sage headed the major institution of learning in an era of political and economic tranquility was not likely to be repeated. He foresaw that the situation of the Jews would eventually deteriorate. Rebbi had witnessed or remembered the end of the period of persecutions that followed the Great Revolt. His thinking was probably motivated by apprehension for the fate of the Oral Torah in another period of calamity.

The Talmud relates how, thanks to the tremendous effort and self-sacrifice of the last sage of that generation to receive *semikha* (ordination), the chain of *semikha* was continued for yet another generation.[6] However, this was a unique, almost miraculous, event, which made the danger to the continued existence of the Oral Torah even more palpable.

6. *Sanhedrin* 14a: "Once the wicked government decreed [as an act of religious persecution] that whoever performed an ordination should be put to death, and whoever received ordination should be put to death, the city in which the ordination took place demolished and the [Shabbat] boundaries wherein it had been performed, uprooted. What did Rabbi Yehuda ben Bava do? He went and sat between two great mountains [that lay] between two large cities: between the [Shabbat] boundaries of the cities of Usha and Shefar'am, and there ordained five sages: Rabbi Meir, Rabbi Yehuda, Rabbi Shimon, Rabbi Yossi, and Rabbi Elazar ben Shamua. Rav Avia added also Rabbi Neḥemia in the list. As soon as their enemies discovered them, he [Rabbi Yehuda ben Bava] urged them: 'My children, flee.' They said to him, 'What will become of you, Rabbi?' 'I lie before them like a stone which no one [is concerned to] overturn,' he replied. It was said that the enemy did not stir from the spot until they had driven three hundred iron spearheads into his body, making it like a sieve."

The continued existence of the Oral tradition is possible only when there is ongoing transmission between master and pupil over many years of study and repetition. Rebbi feared for the future of Jewish settlement in the Land of Israel and was concerned lest the Oral Torah be splintered among different *batei midrash* and incompatible traditions. If it would be impossible to restore unity under such conditions, then the total rupture of the Oral Torah tradition would be inevitable. Therefore, and despite the fact that this would mean undermining its foundations, Rebbi decided that the time had come to mold the Oral Torah into a single, fixed, and written framework.

Sages of the previous generation had already taken steps in that direction. Rabbi Akiva had apparently gathered various traditions and organized them in some kind of fixed format.[7] His disciple, Rabbi Meir, even formulated the matrix text which served as the basis for the text of the Mishna.[8] Rebbi took this raw material, which had been fashioned and collected orally from various *batei midrash* and traditions of the generations following the Great Revolt – some of them contradictory, others barely represented – and cast them into a single mold: the halakha of the Oral Torah.

The restrictive format of the Mishna could not hold all the material of the Oral Torah. Not all the traditions, disputes, and differences in approach could be represented. It was necessary to omit a great deal of material, to merge various positions, and to arrange legal structures and traditions into uniform expository sequences. The tremendous enterprise of establishing a format for structuring conclusive halakha into a Mishna, which was to be handed down to subsequent generations, entailed a massive amount of clarification and research. The different

7. *Avot deRabbi Natan* 18: "What can Rabbi Akiva be compared to? He can be likened to a worker who takes his box and goes outside. If he finds wheat, he puts it there; if he finds barley, he puts it there; and so he does also with spelt, beans, and lentils. When he returns home, he sorts them, putting wheat separately, barley separately, spelt separately, beans separately, lentils separately. This is how Rabbi Akiva sorted out the entire Torah."
8. *Sanhedrin* 86a: "An anonymous mishna is Rabbi Meir; an anonymous *tosefta*, Rabbi Neḥemia; an anonymous [dictum in the] *Sifra*, Rabbi Yehuda; in the *Sifrei*, Rabbi Shimon; and all are taught according to the views of Rabbi Akiva."

versions and approaches had to be compared, and a decision had to be made regarding the normative principle that would determine the direction of the huge mass of halakhic rulings. Although it is not clear whether Rebbi actually committed the Mishna to writing, it is clear that he produced a record, even if only an oral one, that is the distillation of an enormous number of traditions (six or seven hundred Orders of Mishna, according to the Talmud). This mass of material had to be reduced to a quantity that could be memorized by anyone, and which could henceforth serve as a basic study text. At the same time, Rebbi continued the tradition of preceding generations, and the Oral Torah continued to develop in his day too, both in terms of clarifying contemporary problems and in terms of what was later to be called "The Talmud" – the collection of the discussions and disputes of the sages and scholars, as they investigated the reasons and rationales for each opinion and method in determining the halakha.

Another aspect of Rabbi's personality, and of the tradition he established for the future, was his special attitude towards the Hebrew language. His home was apparently one of the last in which Hebrew (as opposed to Aramaic) was the spoken language of everyday use. It is said that the sages would go to Rebbi's maidservant to learn the meaning of Hebrew words which were no longer known even by the scholars in the *beit midrash*.[9] As part of the tradition he established for future generations, Rebbi expressed his keen care for language in the unique phrasing he used in the Mishna. For in addition to the tremendous task of clarifying and determining the contents, the editing of the Mishna entailed the most important work of phrasing. Incorporating the opinions of various sages, who had lived in various times and places, into one unified structure, produced a variety of linguistic forms in the Mishna, including more ancient strata of the language – dating back to the beginning of the Second Temple era – as well as the different dialects spoken in Jerusalem, Judea, and the Galilee. Rebbi's task was to forge a unified

9. *Rosh HaShana* 26b: "The Rabbis did not know what was meant by [the Hebrew word] *serugin*, till one day they heard the maidservant of Rebbi's household, on seeing the Rabbis enter at intervals, say to them: 'How long are you going to come in by *serugin*?'"

idiom and to determine fixed terminology for the course of a *sugya,* as well as set the basic vocabulary of the halakha, all of which were to serve for generations. In addition, Rebbi had to make sure that this system, despite its extreme terseness, would be precise, comprehensible, and easy to repeat and memorize.

This enormous enterprise – in terms of both form and content – was eventually formulated into a book which, albeit small in quantity, became the central legal codex of the Jewish people. Some say that the Mishna is called "Mishna" (lit., "secondary") because it is second only to the Written Torah, just as the viceroy is second to the king. Indeed, the relationship between the Torah and the Mishna has become the main relationship between the Law of the Written Torah and the clearly phrased, forged halakha of the Oral Torah. From Rebbi's time onward through the Talmudic era and to this very day, the Mishna has consistently retained its place. Rebbi's work has survived not as a private, temporary enterprise, but as a work which set the pattern for the Torah of the Jewish people throughout the ages. The title "Rebbi," bestowed on him in his lifetime, therefore remains valid for all generations to come.

Chapter eight

Rav

Rabbi Abba bar Aivo, known in the Talmud as "Rav," is ranked first and foremost among the Babylonian amoraim.

There were important scholars in Babylonia prior to him, and an extensive network of Torah-study frameworks upon which Rav himself drew. Until Rav's advent, however, Babylonian scholarship was regarded as subsidiary to that of the Land of Israel. Rav's arrival in Babylonia marks the beginning of spiritual independence for Babylonian Jewry, the building of its great yeshivot and the start of the Babylonian Talmud. While this magnum opus had many authors throughout the generations, it might not have come into being at all – and would surely have been different in scope – were it not for the contribution of Rav's personality and scholarship.

Rav was born in Babylonia, yet he acquired most of his learning and traditions in the Land of Israel. In his youth he followed his uncle, Rabbi Ḥiyya the Great, to the Land of Israel and studied along with him under Rabbi Yehuda HaNasi ("Rebbi"). Although among the youngest disciples in Rebbi's *beit midrash*, he was even then one of the judges in Rebbi's *beit din*.[1] He had a particularly close personal relationship with

1. *Gittin* 59a: "Rav said: I was in the Assembly of Rebbi, and my vote was taken first."

Rebbi, as did others of his family who were considered part of the *Nasi*'s household.

Rav learned Torah from some of Rebbi's colleagues and preeminent disciples as well[2]; in addition, he received the essence of Babylonian scholarship from Rabbi Ḥiyya.[3] A Jewish center had been in existence in Babylonia since the destruction of the First Temple. As an independent entity it had, in the course of time, developed its own study methods. These principles and concepts were still in embryonic form, and certainly could not compete with those of the great center in the Land of Israel. Yet, as unrefined and undefined as they were, Rabbi Ḥiyya crystallized them and transmitted them to Rav.

Since Rav's activity began at the end of the Mishnaic period, he is considered a transitory figure between the tannaim and amoraim. The Babylonian Talmud accepts the assumption (infrequently mentioned, but always in the background) that Rav "was a tanna and could differ" (*Eruvin* 50b; *Ketubot* 8a; *Gittin* 38b; *Bava Batra* 42a; *Sanhedrin* 83b; *Ḥulin* 122b). In other words, Rav's status was beyond that of an amora, who merely explicates tanna statements, and akin to that of a tanna, who could dispute statements of other tannaim and even the Mishna itself. Some believe that the tanna "Rabbi Abba," who appears in several *baraitot*, is really Rav, referred to by his true name, Rabbi Abba (*Ketubot* 81a, and see also the *Arukh*, entry "Rav").

Rav came from a distinguished Babylonian family, related to the exilarch and tracing its lineage to the House of David.[4] There were renowned and important Torah scholars in his family, such as his father Rabbi Aivo, and his uncle and teacher Rabbi Ḥiyya the Great. A special affinity developed between Rav and Rabbi Ḥiyya[5] who was, through

2. Among them: Rav Yitzḥak bar Avdimi, Summakhos, Rabbi Elazar ben Rabbi Shimon, Rabban Gamliel (Rebbi's son), and others.
3. *Bereshit Raba* 33:3: "During all the thirty days that Rabbi Ḥiyya was reprimanded by Rebbi, he taught Rav, his nephew, all the rules of Torah [study] according to the Babylonian [method]."
4. From *Ketubot* 62b it can be understood that he was a descendant of David's brother Shim'i; and from the Jerusalem Talmud, *Ta'anit* 4:2, it can be inferred that he was a descendant of David himself.
5. See *Bava Kama* 99b; *Eruvin* 73a; *Berakhot* 43a; Jerusalem Talmud, *Sanhedrin* 3:6; and elsewhere.

an odd coincidence, the brother of both his father and his mother (see *Sanhedrin* 5a). The uncle doted on his nephew and tried to elevate him above his peers. Rav, for his part, subsequently defended this uncle's halakhic methodology.

With the deaths of Rebbi and Rabbi Ḥiyya, there was no longer an influential and authoritative figure in the Land of Israel from whom Rav could study. A drawn-out personal feud, while essentially inconsequential, additionally complicated Rav's continued residence there.[6] Rav was trapped in an ambiguous position: for family and other reasons he could not assume leadership in the Land of Israel; on the other hand, he was already too prominent to remain a disciple.

Although Rav was compelled to return to Babylonia, in retrospect it is clear that the benefit went far beyond the personal: Rav's presence was the seminal factor in Babylonian scholarship. Worthy of a leadership role in Rebbi's stead, Rav settled in a land which lay fallow in the Torah sense. There he planted what he had already mastered and developed – a new, unique center.

In Babylonia, Rav encountered circumstances similar to those he had left behind in the Land of Israel. Babylonia was not a vacuum either: important scholars, such as the distinguished Shmuel and Karna, already lived there, as did Rav Shela, head of the *beit midrash* at Neharde'a.[7] Despite his credentials, Rav chose not to enter into a confrontation with the local veteran scholars. He therefore left Neharde'a for Sura, which

6. *Yoma* 87a: "Once Rav was expounding portions of the Bible before Rabbis, and there entered Rabbi Ḥiyya, whereupon Rav started again from the beginning; as Rabbi Shimon, the son of Rebbi, entered, he started again from the beginning. But when Rabbi Ḥanina bar Ḥama entered, he said: So often shall I go back? And he did not go over it again. Rabbi Ḥanina took that amiss. Rav went to him on thirteen eves of the Day of Atonement, but he would not be pacified. But how could he do so?… Rabbi Ḥanina had seen in a dream that Rav was being hanged on a palm tree, and since the tradition is that one who in a dream is hanged on a palm tree will become head [of an Academy], he concluded that authority will be given to him, and so he would not be pacified, with the result that he [Rav] departed to teach Torah in Babylonia."
7. On their meeting with Rav upon his arrival in Babylonia, see *Shabbat* 108a, and *Yoma* 20b.

was near his birthplace Kafri; and there, where there were no existing *batei midrash*, he established one of his own.

The sages describe Rav's arrival in Sura thus: "Rav found an open field and put up a fence around it" (*Eruvin* 100b). In other words, Rav came to a cultural wilderness and constructed a great and perfect edifice. His *beit midrash* in Sura not only became the most important one in Babylonia at the time, but remained a Torah center for over eight hundred years, longer than any other yeshiva. Throughout the Talmudic period and for generations thereafter – in effect, until the end of the Geonic period – the Sura yeshiva continued as one of the two greatest Babylonian Torah centers. It was the only center that did not move from its physical location and, to a great degree, it also remained loyal to its original methodology.

Unlike the other yeshivot that were more Babylonian in style, the Sura yeshiva – despite being an independent Babylonian establishment – was deeply linked, emotionally and scholastically, to the Land of Israel. Its methodology was characterized by a tendency to *peshat* on one hand, and to *Midrash Aggada* and the esoteric on the other, similar to the dialectic of study in the Land of Israel.

The final editing of the Talmud by Rav Ashi, who was the head of the Sura yeshiva generations later, closed a circle begun by Rav, the founder of that yeshiva. The interchanges between Rav and his colleagues, and Rav and his disciples, formed the main corpus upon which the Talmud was built; many generations later, it was disciples of Rav's disciples who completed the enterprise. The underlying approach, which made it possible to create and to complete this gigantic opus, was Rav's Israel-rooted approach: the striving to take things beyond a splendid start towards a resolution, to reach conclusions, and to establish defined study methods without sinking into endless *pilpul*.

Rabbi Abba bar Aivo was not called by his name, but by the appellation "Rav," because he was the Rabbi of Diaspora Jewry (see Rashbam on *Pesaḥim* 119b). Even scholars and study houses that neither followed his method nor studied Torah directly from him, were influenced by him indirectly. In building an influential center in Babylonia, Rav was scrupulously careful not to undermine the scholars and *batei midrash* that preceded him. He made room for differing opinions, even those of sages who were prepared to accept his authority such as Shmuel and Rav Shela. In fact, the controversies and interchanges between Rav and his colleague Shmuel (known afterwards as "*Havayot deRav uShmuel*") constitute the primary basis for the discourses in the Babylonian Talmud. The Talmud's almost dualistic system – of two *batei midrash* or two scholars respectfully disputing one another – was largely a consequence and a continuation of Rav's technique, which neither wished nor attempted to destroy other opinions or alternative approaches.

Although we sometimes find Rav imposing his authority upon one individual or another,[8] the overall figure that emerges from the many stories about him is full of refinement and gentleness, both as an individual and in his relationships with family members and others (see *Yevamot* 63a; *Bava Metzia* 59a; and elsewhere). He felt obligated to relate respectfully even to those of lesser stature, and was ready to take criticism from students and peers. Often, he would avoid responding to questions or criticism raised against him as if he had no answer, although his replies to many of those same issues are to be found in other places. Rav granted everyone, including those close to him, the opportunity to distinguish themselves, and gave each individual room to speak and act as suited his nature.

Rav was also famous for his personal sanctity. This found expression in the titles bestowed upon him by his students: "Our holy Rabbi," or "Our great Rabbi, may the Almighty help him" (*Sukka* 33a). Both in keeping with the tradition of his family, who were renowned as saintly people, and with the tradition of the Land of Israel (which he received mainly from Rebbi), Rav conducted himself with great asceticism – which, however, he applied to himself alone. There is a list of ten pious customs undertaken by Rav,[9] among them that he was never without

8. E.g., *Yevamot* 52a: He would flog whoever would betroth a woman by sexual intercourse, or in the open street, or without previous negotiation. Ibid., 45a: Rav fixed his eyes upon a certain man, and he died. *Megilla* 5b: He cursed a person who sowed on Purim; Jerusalem Talmud, *Nedarim* 9:20, and elsewhere.
9. In *Teshuvot HaGeonim, Sha'arei Teshuva* 178, we find the full list, which is: 1. He never raised his eyes from the ground; 2. He never went bare-headed; 3. He ate three meals on Shabbat; 4. He never glanced aside; 5. He never looked ahead; 6. He would go in a roundabout way, so as not to trouble the community (by making them rise

tzitzit and tefillin, and that he never raised his eyes from the ground. In later generations, many who tried to copy even a single detail from the complex of his activities and his way of life often fell to severe extremism.

Rav also had the singular ability to attract students. It seems that Rav was the first to create the institution of the yeshiva in Babylonia in such unprecedented scope and quality. Most of Rav's students became the leaders and outstanding figures of the following generation. The creation of this group, moreover, enabled and encouraged the creation of parallel groups in other places.

The model of the yeshiva created by Rav was both similar and dissimilar to the original model in the Land of Israel. While in the Land of Israel the yeshiva relied on its proximity to the *beit din* or to the Great *Sanhedrin,* in Babylonia other frameworks created an independent tradition and were the basis of the yeshiva's existence. One of these was the *yarḥei kalla* – the two yearly sessions in which scholars from all over the country would assemble for a month of intensive Torah study. In the five months between those sessions, the participating scholars would study on their own, or prepare the material to be dealt with at the next month of intensive study. This pattern became routine in Babylonia from Rav's time onward, and it continued as long as there was Torah study there. It facilitated the inclusion of a great number of people in very concentrated Torah study while at the same time creating a structure for Torah study that was not geared to professional scholars alone.

Rav strove to create a yeshiva that would be based on students who were highly skilled in Torah study, even though each had his own occupation, which took most of his time. Thus the institution of *yarhei kallah,* which existed before Rav, acquired full validity, force, and significance in his day, and served as the model for all the Babylonian yeshivot for successive generations.

to their feet in his honor); 7. He never ate a meal unless it was connected with the fulfillment of a mitzva; 8. He went to appease whoever provoked him; 9. He had a pleasant voice, and he would serve both as leader in prayer and as interpreter; 10. He always wore tzitzit and tefillin.

Chapter nine

Shmuel

Rav and Shmuel were the first of the pairs of scholars among the amoraim who created the Babylonian Talmud. Rav and Shmuel were antithetical in personality and in outward appearance. Rav was a tall and impressive figure, nicknamed Abba *Arikha* – "Abba the tall" (*Ḥulin* 137b). Of Shmuel's appearance we have the rather irreverent description by a woman: "He is short and big-stomached, dark and large-teethed."[1] Despite all that, and although they came from different backgrounds, worked independently, and their period of collaboration was brief, in the minds of the generations they remain a pair. Their controversies, known as *Ḥavayot deRav uShmuel* (*Berakhot* 19b), like the *Havayot deAbaye veRava* in a later period, are the building blocks of the Babylonian Talmud.

Shmuel was one of the most exceptional figures among the great

1. *Nedarim* 50b: "A certain woman of Neharde'a came before Rav Yehuda [at Pumbedita] for a lawsuit, and was declared guilty by the court. 'Would your teacher Shmuel have judged thus?' she said. 'Do you know him, then?' he asked. 'Yes. He is short and big-stomached, dark and large-toothed.' 'What, you have come to insult him! Let that woman be under the ban!' he exclaimed. She burst and died."

variety of types of tannaim and amoraim. He was a distinguished scholar and head of a yeshiva who left his mark for many generations. Yet, unlike Rav and many other colleagues, he was the first Babylonian scholar to have never officially been ordained and he never bore the title "Rabbi." Thus, Shmuel started a tradition of scholars who did not receive formal recognition of status from the center in the Land of Israel.

Why Shmuel was never ordained may be due not only to technical reasons,[2] but also to his family history. Shmuel was a descendant of the tanna Ḥanania (Rabbi Yehoshua ben Ḥanania's nephew), who, two generations earlier, tried to create an independent center of scholarship in Babylonia parallel to that in the Land of Israel (*Berakhot* 63a; Jerusalem Talmud, *Nedarim* 6:8). Ḥanania's effort failed, but "Ḥanania's offense" (as it was subsequently known) was neither forgotten nor forgiven even in the generations that followed.

Unlike Rav, who spent a significant portion of his life in the Land of Israel, Shmuel was a preeminent product of the Babylonian school. Opinion is divided as to whether Shmuel was ever in the Land of Israel (*Bava Metzia* 85b). Those who believe that Shmuel was there claim that he managed to study with Rabbi Yehuda HaNasi ("Rebbi") and to serve as his personal physician. Rebbi esteemed Shmuel as a physician and as a scholar and tried to ordain him as a rabbi. However, he did not find a suitable opportunity to do so. When the ordination was repeatedly postponed, Shmuel made the following comment: "I have seen the Book of Adam, in which is written, 'Shmuel *Yarḥina'a* (lunar expert, or astronomer)[3] shall be called '*Ḥakim*,' but not 'Rabbi'" (ibid.). This statement is ambiguous, since the word *Ḥakim* means both scholar and physician.

As was common among men of science in those times, Shmuel was also an astronomer. If Shmuel is indeed "Shmuel *Yarḥina'a*," the title attests to his erudition in celestial affairs. Shmuel himself remarked that

2. He may have been in Israel for too short a time or at a period when the ordaining body, the *Sanhedrin*, was not convened, etc.
3. There are differences of opinion as to whether "Shmuel *Yarḥina'a*" mentioned here is indeed the great amora Shmuel or a different person, who is mentioned once only, in this source.

he was as familiar with the paths of the heavens as with the streets of his city Neharde'a (*Berakhot* 58b). Among the Jewish scholars of the day, however, being both a physician and an astronomer was quite unusual. While most Torah scholars did work for a living, most were farmers; whereas Shmuel lived in a cosmopolitan commercial center and was affiliated with the wider world of the sciences.

Rabbi Yoḥanan's letters to the Babylonian scholars tell us a great deal about how the Israel scholars thought of Shmuel. The leading scholar in the Land of Israel, Rabbi Yoḥanan, was younger than Rav and Shmuel. During Rav's lifetime, Rabbi Yoḥanan opened his letters with the greeting, "To our Rabbis in Babylonia." After Rav's death, when Shmuel effectively took his place, Rabbi Yoḥanan would write, "To our colleagues in Babylonia." To persuade Rabbi Yoḥanan that he, too, ought to be addressed with the title "Our Rabbi," Shmuel sent him a sixty-year calendar. Rabbi Yoḥanan was not impressed in the least and merely observed that Shmuel was obviously a proficient mathematician. Only much later did Shmuel succeed in convincing Rabbi Yoḥanan that he was not only a wise man, but a Torah scholar as well (*Ḥulin* 95b).

Shmuel's medical practice and his studies in astronomy (and to an extent also astrology) brought him into close contact with non-Jewish scholars. Among his Gentile friends was a Babylonian scholar called Avlet (perhaps a shortened version of the name Obalit). Their discussions on astronomy, philosophy, and general world affairs are recorded in the Talmud (*Shabbat* 129a; 156a; *Avoda Zara* 30a). Shmuel also frequented the debating societies in his city, where religious and philosophical issues were discussed. Although Rav, too, had broad horizons, he would never set foot in such places.

In his ability to build close personal friendships without standing on ceremony, Shmuel resembled his father. Both cared about principles and essentials and not about personal status. In the Jerusalem Talmud, Shmuel's father is referred to by his proper name, Abba bar Abba. However, the Babylonian Talmud refers to him almost only as "Shmuel's father" (Avuh diShmuel). Shmuel was such an outstanding personality that his father – an important scholar in his own right, whose opinions and honor were deferred to even by scholars in the Land of Israel (*Bava Metzia* 90a; *Yevamot* 105a) – was relegated to the shadows by comparison.

Shmuel had very close ties to the household of the exilarch. The exilarch in his time, Mar Ukba, was a gentle and unassuming man, involved in charity and compassionate deeds. Perhaps this accounts for their mutual affinity. The exilarch was not then accorded the special status he later acquired when the government recognized his formal position as Prince of the Jews. Still, he did enjoy considerable authority, even in the area of civil law. Shmuel's close ties with the exilarch made him more familiar with Babylonian Jewry's judicial system than many other scholars were. Although he did not have the official standing (not yet created) of the Exilarch's Advisor ("*Ḥakham Rosh HaGola*"), he was the closest person to the exilarch and to his judicial system.

Shmuel was thus better acquainted than others with the various areas of civil law, from property to torts. It was with good reason that issues of religious law were determined according to Rav, while Shmuel decided the halakha relating to monetary issues (*Bekhorot* 49b). Scholars of succeeding generations realized that Rav had the ability to encompass the Babylonian and Israeli traditions and mold them into an integrated system; but that in monetary matters and everyday practical issues, Shmuel's proficiency was the greater. In this sense, Rav was the theoretician while Shmuel was the practical man of law. Generally speaking, Shmuel's experience in the real world, both as a doctor and as a judge, gave him better understanding of social and personal problems.

In disputes between Rav and Shmuel, Shmuel almost always represents the perspective that derives from existential reality. He sees the problems of the world as they are seen and sensed by others. A dispute between Rav and Shmuel in explicating a verse from the Book of Esther is an apt example (*Megilla* 13a): The guard in charge of Ahasuerus's harem "favored Esther for the good" over all the other women (Esther 2:9). Rav says that he favored her by giving her kosher food; Shmuel says that he favored her by giving her pork chops. Rav's concept of good is clear: good means kosher, correct, proper. Shmuel, on the other hand, could see things from the perspective of the Gentile guard. What would such a guard consider good? How would he favor the young lady with a chance to be chosen queen? He would definitely give her pork chops. This difference in approach, which illuminates the deep polarities in their natures, is found in many other disputes between them on topics that are much more grave and serious.

The personal relationship between Rav and Shmuel was a rather tangled one. Rav sensed that his very arrival in Babylonia created a new center of gravity, by definition an injustice to Shmuel. He therefore compensated by according him great honor. With all that, Rav may have underestimated the power and the talents which lay behind Shmuel's self-effacement. From the time of Rav and Shmuel, the Babylonian yeshivot developed along two separate lines, concentrating around the two great centers. There was the yeshiva founded by Rav and based upon his traditions in Sura. Alongside it was the yeshiva which continued Shmuel's method, first situated in Neharde'a and later, after being destroyed in the many wars between Persia and Rome, moved (or rather, most of its sages moved) to Pumbedita. The yeshivot at Sura and Pumbedita, throughout the hundreds of years of their existence, were very much linked to the personalities of the two individuals who headed them: Rav – the founder of the former yeshiva, and Shmuel, the head of the latter.

Throughout the generations, the yeshiva at Sura was always more "Israeli" in its strong link to the Torah study methods and the scholars of the Land of Israel. It was characterized by comprehensive definitions and all-encompassing summations, along with a bent for the esoteric and the Kabbala. The yeshiva at Pumbedita, on the other hand, perpetuated Shmuel's method and was more distinctively Babylonian. Its scholars were less interested in the large scopes and broad problems of classification, and more engaged in hair-splitting analysis, and in the world and its problems. Their minds were also more open to general knowledge and to the universe outside the yeshiva walls.

Rav, like many of his generation, could not properly appreciate Shmuel's strength for he was modest, reticent, and unassuming. Shmuel nonetheless never relinquished his opinion or altered his basic approach. Quietly and unobtrusively, he refrained from disputes liable to lead to divisiveness or agitation. Avoiding confrontation, he built a complete and unique school of thought.

Shmuel was younger than Rav and outlived him. After Rav's death, many of his former students gathered around Shmuel and were nourished by his unique halakhic methodology as well as by his affinity with real life.

Shmuel had no sons. His students and their students, who perpetuated his method throughout all the generations in which the Talmud was formed, imprinted in it Shmuel's approach which, perhaps even more than Rav's, characterizes the inner essence of the Babylonian Talmud.

Chapter ten

Rabbi Yoḥanan

Rabbi Yoḥanan was the greatest of the amoraim in the Land of Israel and undoubtedly one of the central figures in all of Talmudic literature. According to tradition, Rabbi Yoḥanan was the editor of the Jerusalem Talmud. Although the amoraim of the Land of Israel continued for several generations after Rabbi Yoḥanan, his character and his work were the central axis of the Jerusalem Talmud. His influence is felt not only in the Jerusalem Talmud, but to a large extent in the Babylonian Talmud as well; both bear the stamp of his sayings and his personality throughout, in halakha and *aggada* alike.

During Rabbi Yoḥanan's era, actually the two generations in which he was active, he was the most important and impressive figure in the entire Jewish world. His teachings, as transmitted directly to students in the Land of Israel, and indirectly to other Jews wherever they lived, were one of the few stable things within the Jewish world, which was then beset with disputes and controversies.

There were those who disputed Rabbi Yoḥanan, too, in his day and subsequently. Nevertheless, in halakhic methodology he was and continued to be the dominant personality, both in the teachings of the Land of Israel and, to a large extent, in halakha in general. In the

Jerusalem Talmud, halakha is nearly always determined according to Rabbi Yoḥanan, and in the final analysis, the same is true in the Babylonian Talmud. The cumulative weight of his personality, backed by the prestige of the Land of Israel, was decisive even against the acclaimed Babylonian amoraim, Rav and Shmuel.

Rabbi Yoḥanan's renown is confirmed by a letter sent to Rabba (Rabba bar Naḥmani, one of the greatest Babylonian amoraim; see chapter 12). Rabba's brothers, who had moved to the Land of Israel, tried to convince him to join them and wrote, "And lest you might think that you have no master [good enough for you here, we can tell you that] you have one, and he is Rabbi Yoḥanan" (*Ketubot* 111a).

Indeed, after the death of Rav and Shmuel many of their disciples moved to the Land of Israel to study Torah from Rabbi Yoḥanan. Some of them stayed in the Land of Israel and their work became characteristically "Israeli"; among them were even some who became so zealous that they scorned their country of origin, considering the Torah of the Land of Israel paramount (*Beitza* 15a and elsewhere). It was said that when Rabbi Zeira arrived in the Land of Israel to study with Rabbi Yoḥanan, he fasted one hundred fasts in order to forget the Babylonian Talmud. He did not want to confuse it with the teachings of the Land of Israel (*Bava Metzia* 85a). Rabbi Yoḥanan himself, however, was not all that dogmatic, and he honored and respected the Babylonian scholars.

Rabbi Yoḥanan lived to a ripe old age. In his youth, he learned in the *beit midrash* of Rabbi Yehuda HaNasi ("Rebbi") (*Pesaḥim* 3b; and see *Ḥulin* 137b [see note on p. 75] ibid., 54a), although he was not regarded as one of his disciples. He was the quintessential student of Rabbi Ḥiyya's great disciples: Rabbi Oshaya and Rabbi Yannai, and Ḥizkiyya the son of Rabbi Ḥiyya, and lived on for another two generations after them. His greatness in Torah learning was already recognized by his teachers, who praised him generously. This enthusiasm was echoed also by his students and his students' students when he served as head of the yeshiva.

Rabbi Yoḥanan's eminence did not come easily. We know nothing of his family other than that he was called, both in his presence and not, *bar nappaḥa*, son of the blacksmith (*Ketubot* 25b; *Bava Metzia* 85b; and elsewhere). We know that in his youth he suffered poverty and almost resolved to leave Torah study and engage in trade in order to support himself.[1] He did inherit some property, but as he told his students on several occasions, "This field was mine, and I sold it in order to study Torah," "This vineyard was mine, and I sold it in order to study Torah," "This orchard of olives was mine, and I sold it in order to study Torah" (*Vayikra Raba* 30:1; *Shir HaShirim Raba* 8:7). He apparently came close to destitution and was saved only when, as the head of the yeshiva, he was provided with an honorable livelihood.

Rabbi Yoḥanan's life was filled with troubles, and not only because of his great poverty. He had ten sons, all of whom died within his lifetime. It was told that he saved a bone (or tooth) of the tenth son, which he would show to anyone who complained of his fate, saying, "This is the bone of my tenth son" (*Berakhot* 5b).

Rabbi Yoḥanan was famous for his superb beauty. He was reputed to be one of the most handsome people to have ever lived. The Talmud used a uniquely poetic metaphor to describe him: "Take a silver goblet as it emerges from the crucible, fill it with the seeds of a red pomegranate, encircle its brim with a chaplet of red roses, and set it between the sun and the shade; its lustrous glow is like Rabbi Yoḥanan's beauty" (*Bava Metzia* 84a).

Universal respect, juxtaposed with personal adversity, led Rabbi Yoḥanan to be particularly sensitive, especially when others repeated his statements without attributing them to him (*Bava Kama* 117a; ibid., 65a; *Bava Metzia* 84a; Jerusalem Talmud, *Berakhot* 2:1; *Shekalim* 2:5). Rabbi Yoḥanan apparently saw his Torah statements as his sole claim

1. *Ta'anit* 21a: "Ilfa and Rabbi Yoḥanan studied together the Torah and they found themselves in great want and they said one to another, 'Let us go and engage in commerce so that in us the verse will be fulfilled: "There shall be no need among you"' (Deuteronomy 15:4). They went and sat down under a ruin of a wall, and while they were having their meal two ministering angels came. Rabbi Yoḥanan overheard one saying to the other, 'Let us throw this wall upon these [people] and kill them, because they forsake etemal life and occupy themselves with temporal life.' The other [angel] replied: 'Leave them alone because one of them has still much to achieve.' Rabbi Yoḥanan heard this but Ilfa did not. Rabbi Yoḥanan asked Ilfa, 'Master, have you heard anything?' He replied: 'No.' Rabbi Yoḥanan said to himself: 'As I heard this and Ilfa has not, it is clear that I am the one who still has much to achieve.' Rabbi Yoḥanan then said to Ilfa: 'I will go back, so that it may be fulfilled, for "The poor shall never cease out of the land"' (ibid., verse 11).

to eternity. He was bereft of all ties to the world, financial and familial; only his Torah study and his disciples could interest him, and they were everything to him.

Rabbi Yoḥanan was totally absorbed in the four cubits of the *beit midrash* and hardly ever left it. This was the world that he had chosen in his youth, and there he remained for all of his long life – as a man of the *beit midrash* who resided in the *beit midrash*. He was not, therefore, a political leader, even though his power and his personality could have been the decisive factor on any issue, and even though all of his contemporaries, from the Babylonian sages to the *Nasi* of the *Sanhedrin* in the Land of Israel, were willing to accept almost every ruling he made.

It was Rabbi Yoḥanan who effectively created the study methodology of the Jerusalem Talmud. His predecessors had still continued Rebbi's work, both by collecting *baraitot* which had not been included in the Mishna, and by putting the finishing textual touches to the Mishna. Rabbi Yoḥanan, on the other hand, was first and foremost among the distinguished amoraim who created the Talmud.

One of Rabbi Yoḥanan's most basic beliefs was in the centrality of the Mishna. He lay down a fundamental rule of halakha – that the law is in accordance with the anonymously recorded Mishna (*Shabbat* 46a; ibid., 81b; *Eruvin* 92a; and elsewhere). All the major decisors, and especially Maimonides, followed him. This, de facto, gave the Mishna special status. In practice, this means that the authoritative decision on the halakha is stated in the Mishna proper, and not in any of the other opinions mentioned elsewhere, either in the Mishna or in the many compilations of tannaitic statements assembled around the Mishna.

While other scholars wanted to broaden the tannaitic base on which the Mishna rested – to reinstate some of the extensive material which Rebbi had left out – Rabbi Yoḥanan went back to the Mishna as written and formulated by Rebbi. Rabbi Yoḥanan also established the rule that whatever was not cited in the Mishna had dubious practical, halakhic value. He used to say: "Rebbi had not taught this ruling; how could Rabbi Ḥiyya know it?" (*Eruvin* 92a; *Yevamot* 43a; and elsewhere). Rabbi Yoḥanan's method returned to the Mishna and focused on it as the primary source from which to learn and draw conclusions. His assertion that "the law follows the anonymous Mishna" permanently established the principle that the predominant halakhic verdicts of the Jewish world remain anchored in the Mishna.

Even though Rabbi Yoḥanan personally enjoyed the debate and *pilpul* of his students, his usual approach tended to the *peshat*. Without sophistry and extraneous inquiry, Rabbi Yoḥanan worked toward an understanding of the meaning of the Mishna as a single, complete unit. His approach was primarily expository. It did not ignore new problems, but tried to link them to the accepted traditions of the Mishna. Against the Babylonian style, which tended to casuistry and sharp-wittedness, Rabbi Yoḥanan's approach (which became the salient method of the Jerusalem Talmud) sought the core of the matter and drove toward understanding, without digressions to side issues or to problems removed from reality. In the Land of Israel, Rabbi Yirmiya was expelled from the *beit midrash* after having raised tangential issues at hand,[2] while in Babylonia such questions would never have resulted in anyone's ouster from the Study Hall.

Also characteristic of the Land of Israel was Rabbi Yoḥanan's attempt to arrive at halakhic summations and conclusions. Rabbi Yoḥanan was therefore careful to rely on clear, authoritative sources; he would not say anything which could not withstand analysis, either textual or academic. Other scholars sought to harmonize the halakha by searching after obscure opinions and trying to reconcile them; Rabbi Yoḥanan wanted to comprehend and to compile that which he knew. He did not exhaustively investigate all the tannaitic sources available. He saw no need to deal with sources which did not fit into the path he had outlined for determining the halakha, the path he took throughout the many years in which he was the Torah leader of the Jewish people.

Rabbi Yoḥanan's relations with other sages of his generation were quite varied. He treated with respect and esteem the Babylonian amora Rav, whom he remembered from the time that he had spent in the Land of Israel,[3] and with the amora Shmuel he corresponded for many years

2. *Bava Batra* 23b. Rabbi Yirmiya raised the question: "If one foot is within fifty cubits and the other beyond, how do we decide?" It was for this that they turned Rabbi Yirmiya out of the *beit midrash*.
3. *Ḥulin* 137b: "I remember when I was sitting before Rebbi, seventeen rows behind

(*Ḥulin* 95b). Disciples of Rav and Shmuel who came to study under Rabbi Yoḥanan, and who later became central pillars of Torah in the Land of Israel, were his source for news from Babylonia. Indeed, from time to time we find Rabbi Yoḥanan marveling at the wisdom of the Babylonian scholars, when he discovered that they had preempted him in arriving at conclusions similar to his.

Rabbi Yoḥanan's relations with his disciples in the Land of Israel were complex. The time he spent in Tiberias as the head of the local *yeshiva*, although economically difficult, was quite comfortable from other aspects, and Rabbi Yoḥanan succeeded in assembling an enormous number of students from all over the Diaspora. His closest disciple, aside from his brother-in-law Resh Lakish, was Rabbi Elazar ben Pedat. Rabbi Elazar was considered the most important transmitter of Rabbi Yoḥanan's teachings. Yet, in the manner of Talmudic sages, he did not nullify himself in front of his great master, and differences of opinion between them are often recorded. The nature of their relationship is apparent from the following incident. Rabbi Elazar stated an innovation of Rabbi Yoḥanan's without attributing it to him. Rabbi Yoḥanan, who was quite sensitive on that issue for reasons of continuity of tradition as well as for personal reasons, was offended by the omission. His students tried to appease him, and Rabbi Yaakov bar Idi said: "Did Yehoshua, then, concerning every word which he said, tell them, 'Thus did Moses tell me'? But the fact is that Yehoshua was sitting and delivering his discourse without mentioning names, and everyone knew that it was the Torah of Moses. So, too, when your disciple Rabbi Elazar sat and delivered his discourse without mentioning names, everyone knew that it was yours."[4]

Rabbi Yoḥanan was very fond of his student Rabbi Elazar and revealed the softer side of his personality to him, as the following story illustrates: "Rabbi Elazar fell ill and Rabbi Yoḥanan went in to visit him.

Rav, seeing sparks of fire leaping from the mouth of Rebbi into the mouth of Rav and from the mouth of Rav into the mouth of Rebbi, and I could not understand what they were saying."

4. *Yevamot* 96b. See also, Jerusalem Talmud, *Shekalim* 2:5 and *Berakhot* 2:1; and *Midrash Shmuel* 19, as in the case of Rabbi Meir who was known to all as the disciple of Rabbi Akiva.

He noticed that he was lying in a dark room, and he bared his arm and light radiated from it. Thereupon he noticed that Rabbi Elazar was weeping, and he said to him: 'Why do you weep? Is it because you did not study enough Torah? Surely we learnt: The one who sacrifices much and the one who sacrifices little have the same merit, provided that the heart is directed to heaven. Is it perhaps lack of sustenance? Not everybody has the privilege to enjoy two tables. Is it perhaps because of [the lack of] children? This is the bone of my tenth son!'" Rabbi Elazar's next statement expresses the essence of their relationship, and in a way, the attitude of an entire generation towards Rabbi Yoḥanan. "He [Rabbi Elazar] replied: 'I am weeping on account of this beauty that is going to rot in the earth.'" In other words, he wept not for himself, but for the beauty of Rabbi Yoḥanan which was destined to decay. Rabbi Yoḥanan said to him: 'On that account you surely have a reason to weep.' And they both wept" (*Berakhot* 5b). For many people, Rabbi Yoḥanan was the embodiment of greatness and beauty. His death and disappearance from the Jewish scene seemed a tragedy of such magnitude, that it was impossible to imagine resuming normal life.

At the end of the above incident, Rabbi Yoḥanan appears as a wonder worker as well. "In the meanwhile he [Rabbi Yoḥanan] said to him: 'Are your sufferings welcome to you?' He replied: 'Neither they nor their reward.' He said to him: 'Give me your hand.' And he gave him his hand and he raised him." Rabbi Yoḥanan extended his hand, and Rabbi Elazar was healed. In other places, too, Rabbi Yoḥanan appears, albeit unobtrusively, as a miracle worker and one who engages in the esoteric. We know of several of his disciples, such as Rabbi Ami and Rabbi Asi, who acquired their knowledge of the esoteric from him.

Chapter eleven

Resh Lakish

Resh Lakish was the nickname for one of the most outstanding amoraim of the Land of Israel, Rabbi Shimon ben Lakish. It may relate to a curious chapter of his life not completely known, and to a personality which was exceptional, even within the colorful gallery of Talmudic figures.

Resh Lakish was distinctively Israeli. He was raised and educated in the Land of Israel, apparently in the city of Tiberias or its vicinity. Although there is no definitive proof, it seems that, in his youth, Resh Lakish was part of the scholarly community and studied Torah from several of the leading sages of the generation.[1] For reasons that are unclear, possibly economic hardship, he temporarily left the scholarly world.

The late third century was a difficult period in the Land of Israel. The Roman authorities began imposing edicts with the aim of evicting Jewish settlers, particularly farmers, from the Land. The burden of taxation (which eventually led to the destruction of the Roman Empire) was especially oppressive for minorities and for individuals who lacked

1. See *Bava Metzia* 84a, *Tosafot* beginning "If you will repent," and also *Eruvin* 65b, *Tosafot* beginning "Resh Lakish."

patronage and were therefore forced to find alternative sources of income. Resh Lakish, renowned for his immense physical strength, apparently could find no other way to support himself than through the most wretched, most dangerous, and perhaps most lucrative occupation of the time: as a gladiator.

Stepping into the stadium not only meant leaving behind the scholarly milieu; in many ways, it meant withdrawing altogether from the world of men. Gladiators existed in a world of their own. Knowing that they could not survive for long in the cruel arena, they lived for the moment, as unbridled as possible. Bloodshed and lawlessness were part of their world, and entering that world meant deserting civilization.

It is not clear where, or for how long, Resh Lakish was a wrestler. Apparently he did it long enough for him to become famous, probably in Caesarea and other locales where there were audiences for such amusements.

The Talmud (*Bava Metzia* 84a) describes how Resh Lakish reformed his ways. Rabbi Yoḥanan, renowned for his beauty, was bathing in the Jordan River. Resh Lakish, who was passing by, saw him and jumped into the water after him. Rabbi Yoḥanan admired Resh Lakish's strength and complimented him, saying, "Your strength should be for Torah"; in other words, a man of your prowess should invest his energy in Torah study. Impressed by Rabbi Yoḥanan's beauty, Resh Lakish replied, "Your beauty should be for women." They made an agreement: Rabbi Yoḥanan promised his sister, as beautiful as he, to Resh Lakish in marriage, and Resh Lakish undertook to repent and devote his energy to Torah study.

Resh Lakish returned to the *beit midrash*. It was soon clear that his spiritual power did not fall short of his physical stamina. He quickly became one of the eminent scholars in the *beit midrash* of Tiberias, then the most important Jewish center in the world. The greatest sages of the entire Jewish world were concentrated there, including many Babylonian scholars who had come to study under Rabbi Yoḥanan.

The reversal in Resh Lakish's personality when he returned to the world of Torah was not surprising. He had always been a man of extremes and continued to be so in his old-new life as well. The Talmud says that, after hearing from Rabbi Yoḥanan that it was forbidden for a man to laugh in this world, Resh Lakish never laughed again (*Berakhot* 31a). It is also told that he would never speak in public with anyone whose trustworthiness or very character were questionable. It was even said that anyone with whom Resh Lakish conversed in the street could get a loan without guarantors (*Yoma* 9b). In later times, the basis for accepting or rejecting certain traditions could be whether or not Resh Lakish had possibly spoken with the particular person who maintained that tradition (ibid.).

Rabbi Yoḥanan and Resh Lakish were a unique pair in the realm of Torah study. Resh Lakish was usually the one to raise objections and challenges and probe the issues at hand. He would pile up questions, textual or theoretical, on almost everything Rabbi Yoḥanan said. In fact, a significant portion of the *sugyot* in both the Jerusalem and the Babylonian Talmuds is based on the controversies of Rabbi Yoḥanan and Resh Lakish. Resh Lakish did not intend to dispute the very basis of Rabbi Yoḥanan's statements, but to more thoroughly investigate and clarify matters, and that was how Rabbi Yoḥanan himself perceived it, too. Indeed, after Resh Lakish's death, Rabbi Yoḥanan was deeply grieved by his absence. To comfort him, the sages sent one of their most astute colleagues, Rabbi Elazar ben Pedat, to fill Resh Lakish's place. Rabbi Elazar would sit before Rabbi Yoḥanan, and as Rabbi Yoḥanan spoke, he would say: "There is a *baraita* which supports you." Said Rabbi Yoḥanan, "Are you like the son of Lakish? When I stated a law, the son of Lakish would raise twenty-four objections and I would give twenty-four answers, which would then lead to a fuller understanding of the law. But you say, 'A *baraita* has been taught which supports you.' Don't I already know that my dicta are right?" (*Bava Metzia* 84a).

On another occasion (Jerusalem Talmud, *Sanhedrin* 2:1), Rabbi Yoḥanan expressed the quality of his relationship with Resh Lakish in a most original way. The event took place after Resh Lakish had given one of his typically sharp discourses and had offended the *Nasi*. The *Nasi* was upset and wanted to imprison Resh Lakish. Resh Lakish fled, absenting himself from the *beit midrash*. The following day, when the *Nasi* asked Rabbi Yoḥanan to say some words of Torah, Rabbi Yoḥanan tried to clap with one hand, meaning that without Resh Lakish he was unable to utter his thoughts and ideas, just as one hand cannot make a clapping sound without the other. He needed Resh Lakish in order to create the *beit midrash* discussions: the ongoing debates, the investigation, and clarification of issues that grow out of the give-and-take and the questions and answers.

Very little is known about Resh Lakish's personal life, even after he reformed. Apparently he married Rabbi Yoḥanan's sister and lived with her for many years.[2] She bore him sons, and his youngest son, "*yanuka deResh Lakish*" ("Resh Lakish's baby") was known, even as a child, for his keen mind (*Ta'anit* 9a). It seems, however, that he did not live long, for we do not find any of Resh Lakish's sons among the scholars of the next generation.

In the many disputes between Rabbi Yoḥanan and Resh Lakish, the halakha was generally determined according to Rabbi Yoḥanan, and it is quite certain that Resh Lakish would have agreed with that principle. Nevertheless, in several areas, halakha was established according to Resh Lakish. In spite of Rabbi Yoḥanan's dominant personality, Resh Lakish appears alongside him not as a reflection or a shadow, but as a Torah personality in his own right. Although he acquired much of his learning from Rabbi Yoḥanan, he learned a great deal from other scholars as well (among them Bar Kappara, Rabbi Asi, Rabbi Oshaya, and Rabbi Yannai) and developed ideas of his own. In addition, there were traditions which he remembered from his youth. Even after his experiences in the outside world, he would refer to them, often in order to differ even with Rabbi Yoḥanan.

Resh Lakish was a remarkable mixture of great personal humility on the one hand, and ideological brilliance and extremism on the other. On a personal level, he was never upset with anyone, even when he was offended; but on matters of principle, he showed partiality to no one. His speeches included harsh statements not only in regard to the masses, but also about the leaders and the mighty men of the period. Just as he was a great wrestler who would never capitulate, so he was later to become a man who fought for his own views, never making concessions about his spiritual essence. Even in his disputes with Rabbi Yoḥanan, Resh Lakish

2. See *Bava Metzia* 84a, and Rashi there, that she was his wife until his death, and also *Ta'anit* 9a, that she outlived him.

maintained an independent stance. He would never show the slightest disrespect to his opponent, but at the same time he would not compromise his own dignity or the personal identity he had built for himself.

The death of Resh Lakish and the subsequent death of Rabbi Yoḥanan closed a chapter in the history of the Jerusalem Talmud and the study of Torah in the Land of Israel. Although the Talmud continued to take shape for several more generations, the brilliance of Torah study in the Land of Israel was dimmed, to be restored only with the renewal of Jewish settlement in the Galilee, approximately a thousand years later. Resh Lakish was among the very last "Israeli" sages (as against the many new immigrants who arrived then in Israel). He was one of those people who create reality and do not merely follow past precedents. And therefore, because he was so very authentic and so profoundly connected to the sources, he could be both critical and creative without being disconnected or estranged.

"Resh Lakish" was a nickname; but unlike the nicknames of other sages, which were usually mere abbreviations of their names, his had additional significance. The name Rabbi Shimon was shortened to the initials 'Resh,' and Lakish was his father's name. But this nickname (which, in Aramaic, means "head, leader,") no doubt hinted to his role as head and leader of a group, and not necessarily of yeshiva students or Torah sages. The name expressed the general esteem towards Resh Lakish as a great man with a history of a leader of ruffians. Thus, although Resh Lakish was indeed well respected and his resolute personality elicited awe, this combination of associations – of his early past on the one hand, and his current scholarly image on the other – made for the unique composite of "Resh Lakish."

One of the few disputes in which halakha was decided according to Resh Lakish was the fundamental controversy over acquisition of usufruct. When one transfers to another the rights to use a certain property, is ownership of the property also transmitted? The controversy, which has a variety of expressions and many halakhic ramifications, touches upon the fundamental understanding of the concept of acquisition. The halakha, according to Resh Lakish, is that acquisition of usufruct is not identical with the acquisition of an object. In other words, possession of an object and use of or benefit from it are two separate things. Possession is one kind of a legal privilege, and the right to use and benefit from possession is a separate kind of privilege. This postulate pertains not to one specific dispute, but to a general understanding of the very notion of acquisition in halakha.

The final and most famous dispute between Rabbi Yoḥanan and Resh Lakish (*Bava Metzia* 84a) has to do with the stage of production at which weapons – such as sword, knife, dagger, or spear – are to be considered complete, and thus capable of becoming ritually impure. In the course of the discussion Rabbi Yoḥanan noted, perhaps half in jest, that "a robber (a reference to Resh Lakish's past) understands his trade," namely, is familiar with the tools or weapons of his trade. Resh Lakish took this as an insult and asked, "And if so, how have you bettered my lot [by bringing me to study Torah]: there [as a robber] I was called Master, and here I am called Master." Rabbi Yoḥanan considered the reaction exaggerated and retorted: "Is it not sufficient that I brought you under the wings of the *Shekhina*?"

This exchange, which by modern standards may not seem all that serious, caused – because of its reference to the past and its reflection upon personal character – a final rupture between Rabbi Yoḥanan and Resh Lakish that had tragic consequences. Resh Lakish died shortly after this incident, and Rabbi Yoḥanan, who felt that it was his anger and asperity that had brought about Resh Lakish's death, could not go on. Deeply contrite, Rabbi Yoḥanan lost his sanity and died of grief for the brother-in-law who was the complement of his personality, for that severe and somber counterpart of his who had highlighted Rabbi Yoḥanan' s own brilliance.

Chapter twelve

Abaye

Abaye was one of the most famous amoraim of the Babylonian Talmud. His real name was Naḥmani; "Abaye" was a nickname from his early years. As an orphan, he knew neither of his parents.[1] Abaye was raised by his father's brother, Rabba bar (=son of) Naḥmani, one of the greatest Babylonian amoraim. Since his uncle did not want to call the child by his own father's name, he called him "Abaye" – "little father." In the course of time, the name "Naḥmani" was nearly forgotten. Except for a few references by his colleague Rava (*Shabbat* 33a, 74a; *Nedarim* 54b; and elsewhere), most everyone used the name that his uncle had given to him.

The life of Abaye, the young orphan, was never happy. His uncle Rabba, although the greatest sage of the time and head of a yeshiva, was very poor and the household suffered real hunger (*Eruvin* 68a; *Mo'ed Katan* 28a; *Megilla* 7b; *Gittin* 37b). Abaye relates that he was once invited to dine in the home of Mari bar Mar, a relative of the exilarch, after he had already had his fill in his uncle's house. A meal was served. When

1. *Kiddushin* 31b: "Rabbi Yoḥanan's father died when his mother conceived him, and his mother died when she bore him. And Abaye was likewise."

he sat and ate and ate whatever was set in front of him, he discovered the aptness of the saying (*Megilla* 7b): "The poor man is hungry and does not know it." Even after his uncle's premature death, when Abaye was on his own and became an important Torah personage, his circumstances remained precarious.

Abaye did not live a long life either. His family – that, according to a tradition, descended from Eli the priest – was cursed with brief life spans (see I Shmuel 2:33) and very few reached old age. Abaye lived to about sixty, and others in the family died even younger.[2] In his family life, too, Abaye knew little happiness. His first wife died young, and he himself passed away shortly after remarrying (*Yevamot* 64b).

While his colleague Rava lived a long life, had scholarly sons, and was always wealthy and successful, Abaye always stood apart as one whose personal life was wretched. In addition, the halakha was never determined according to his opinion except for six cases.[3]

Abaye's life revolved in two orbits. The first was his relationship with his uncle and preeminent teacher. Although the Talmud does not provide much in the way of intimate descriptions, it seems that the bond between Abaye and Rabba, who was like a father to him, was one of great love and mutual esteem. Yet the uncle was so revered by Abaye, that (both in his presence and otherwise) he never addressed him by his proper name, but only as "Mar" – namely, "Sir." And it is probably Rabba's wife whom Abaye often cites, saying, "Mother said to me" (*Eruvin* 29b, 65a, 66b, 133b, 134a, and elsewhere). She is the source for

2. *Rosh Hashana* 18a: "Rabba and Abaye were of the house of Eli. Rabba, who devoted himself to the Torah, lived for forty years; Abaye, who devoted himself both to the Torah and to charitable deeds, lived for sixty years."
3. *Sanhedrin* 27a, and elsewhere. Halakha is determined according to Rava, except for six cases in which the law is established according to Abaye's opinion. The six cases are referred to by the mnemonic יע״ל קג״ם in which the letters stand for various legal terms. י stands for יאוש, abandonment of a lost article (*Bava Metzia* 21b); ע stands for עד זומם, a scheming witness (referred to here, in *Sanhedrin* 27a, and in *Bava Kama* 72b); ל stands for לחי העומד מאליו, a pole put up accidentally (*Eruvin* 15a); ק stands for קידושין שלא נמסרו לביאה, betrothal which cannot result in actual cohabitation (*Kiddushin* 51a); ג stands for גילוי דעת בגיטין, the act of revealing one's attitude indirectly in regard to a bill of divorce (*Gittin* 34a); מ stands for מומר, an apostate or open opponent of Jewish law (referred to here, in *Sanhedrin* 27a).

many folk sayings which appear in the Talmud: tales of miracles, stories about devils, remedies, and medications. Thus, in spite of the poverty and tribulations,[4] the family circle of Rabba, Rabba's wife, and Abaye was a very close one. This was one sphere of Abaye's life.

The second was his relationship with his other teacher, Rav Yosef.[5] Rav Yosef was Rabba's rival, colleague, and partner in halakha. Abaye's rapport with Rav Yosef was quite different from his relationship with Rabba. Towards Rabba he felt, as we said, boundless respect and admiration – although, in the manner of Talmudic study, he did not always accept all of Rabba's statements. There were times when he questioned or even refuted them. His relationship with his other teacher, Rav Yosef, was more complex. Rav Yosef himself was very different from Rabba: his personality was milder, and he employed a different study method. While Rabba was known as "one who uproots mountains," Rav Yosef was called "Sinai" – namely, one who retains traditions and is extraordinarily erudite. Thus, although Abaye was Rav Yosef's student, he was a close student, one who stimulates his teacher's thought and often poses questions and raises objections. With Rav Yosef, Abaye was not only a passive recipient, but also gave of his bounty to others. Moreover, towards the end of his life, Rav Yosef lost his eyesight and suffered from a prolonged illness which resulted in partial memory loss. In those years he relied a great deal on Abaye, who would continue and often complement his statements.[6] Rav Yosef was aware of his illness[7] and took Abaye's remarks in good spirit.

4. *Mo'ed Katan* 28a: "At Rabba's house there were sixty bereavements."
5. In a discussion about rising to show honor to one's teacher (*Kiddushin* 33a), Abaye maintained that for a preeminent teacher one must rise as soon as the teacher comes into sight. He himself used to rise as soon as he saw the ear of Rav Yosef's donkey approaching.
6. More than once, Rav Yosef says: "I did not hear that reported ruling," and Abaye corrects him, saying: "You yourself told us that ruling…." (*Eruvin* 10a, 41a, 66b, 73a, 89b; *Nedarim* 41a; and elsewhere).
7. E.g., in regard to the verse, "…the first tablets which you did break, and you shall put them in the ark" (Deuteronomy 10:2), "Rav Yosef learnt: This teaches us that both the tablets and the fragments of the tablets were deposited in the ark. Hence we learn that a scholar who has forgotten his learning through no fault of his, must not be treated with disrespect" (*Menaḥot* 99a).

The generation after Rabba and Rav Yosef can undoubtedly be called "the generation of Abaye and Rava." This pair was one of the most famous pairs in the Talmud, and their disputes – known as *Havayot deAbaye veRava* – were considered by subsequent generations as the very essence of the Talmud. Indeed, in many ways these controversies constitute the core of Talmudic discussion, since they relate to practically all the questions that appear in the Talmud.[8]

The disputes of Abaye and Rava number in the hundreds and are strewn throughout the Talmud. Because they cover such a broad range of topics and areas, it is difficult to outline a consistent pattern to them. They apparently stem from different reasoning, as well as from reliance upon variant sources.

Nevertheless, there are broad themes underlying the views of each scholar, even if at times they appear self-contradictory. One of the most famous disputes between Abaye and Rava has to do with *ye'ush she-lo mi-da'at* ("unconscious abandonment of hope," in the case of a lost object that was found before its owner became aware of the loss; *Bava Metzia* 21b). Abaye and Rava question at what point a person is regarded as having abandoned hope of retrieving a lost article. Is it from the moment that the article is lost or only from the minute that the owner becomes aware of the loss? This specific discussion has important ramifications for all the laws pertaining to objects lost and found, and it determines the approach to such fundamental questions as what is a lost item, and from what point is a lost item considered ownerless.

Underlying this controversy is the basic issue of retroactivity in halakha. Rava, who maintains that there can be *ye'ush she-lo mi-da'at* – namely, that the owner is regarded as having abandoned hope of retrieval from the moment the article is lost, even before becoming aware of the loss – maintains that in this case, there is retroactivity; Abaye, who claims that there cannot be *ye'ush she-lo mi-da'at*, says that abandonment

8. This was true to such an extent, that when the Talmud (*Sukka* 28a) wanted to say that the tanna Rabban Yoḥanan ben Zakkai was proficient in all the laws of the Torah and did not leave a single matter, great or small, unstudied, it says anachronistically that he was proficient in the *Ḥavayot deAbaye veRava*.

of hope must be a defined, conscious act and consequently holds that in this case, there can be no retroactive applicability.

Abaye's and Rava's stances in this controversy are not typical, since in other disputes, which seemingly should lead to similar conclusions, their positions are reversed. For example, in the case of a scheming witness[9] (*Bava Kama* 72b; *Sanhedrin* 27a), Abaye accepts that there can be retroactive disqualification of testimony and rules that a scheming witness is retroactively disqualified. Rava, on the other hand, claims that disqualification cannot apply retroactively, but only from the point at which a legal decision was made.

This seeming contradiction in Abaye's positions in the above two cases should not, however, surprise us. The differences between Abaye and Rava are not only legalistic in nature, but are rooted in their respective worldviews as well. In general, Abaye's approach tends to be legalistic, while Rava's is realistic. Abaye tries, in almost all cases, to present issues from the structural point of view. In this, the predominant influence is not that of his uncle Rabba, but of his teacher Rav Yosef, the man of phenomenal memory and precisely transmitted traditions.

Abaye follows both Rav Yosef's method and desire to preserve the entirety of ancient tradition as well as his formal approach to that tradition. He does not necessarily see legal principles in terms of their impact on the community, but mainly as pure juridical entities. In this he is totally consistent, both when this calls for retroactive applicability and when it does not. This is why he maintains that a scheming witness's testimony is invalidated retroactively from the very moment that he lies, and not from the time that the court declares it false. He thinks that false testimony is inherently invalid, regardless of anybody's awareness of its falsehood. Similarly, Abaye declares a lost object to be ownerless only from the moment when the owner becomes aware of the loss and despairs of finding it; renunciation of an article depends upon the owner's awareness of the loss and not on the time when it was actually lost.

In both these controversies, Abaye's approach is not pragmatic:

9. Witnesses who gave false testimony and are found out. It is a Torah commandment to do to them what they schemed to do to the person against whom they gave false testimony (Deuteronomy 19:16–19).

his acceptance of retroactivity (in the case of a scheming witness) is liable to result in a breakdown of the entire system of testimony, while his rejection of retroactivity (in the case of lost objects) makes it virtually impossible for a finder to keep his find, since it is so very difficult to prove conclusively that the owner has despaired. In both cases we see that for Abaye, halakhic definitions must be precise, and that it is irrelevant for him whether or not they are workable in real life.

In these two particular cases, halakha was established according to Abaye; but in the broad scope of their controversies, Rava's more complex definitions are preferred over Abaye's formalistic conceptions. Rava, in his pragmatic approach, adapts the law to real-life considerations that are always present, even when not stated explicitly, and bridges the discrepancies between law and reality.

Abaye, too, sees the same problems. Yet, unlike Rava, he does not attempt to reconcile contradictions. For him, every legal issue is an entity unto itself, and halakhic rulings are nearly perfect, autonomous definitions. Abaye is not troubled by the practical and theoretical problems created by his approach. He leaves to others all the questions of legal logic and social implications, because – like a *kohen* – he is exclusively interested in preserving basic principles in their most pristine, pure form. For that reason, Abaye is willing to accept things which other scholars find unacceptable, such as variant textual readings, discrepancies in the approach of one individual, or inconsistencies in halakhic position. It is because he perceives each instance as an independent entity and is not all that interested in creating a coherent and encompassing worldview.

The relationship between Abaye and Rava is characterized by profound personal affinity despite vast differences in outlook. This emerges clearly from their personal lives, from their portraits as sketched in the Talmud, and from the Torah which they bequeathed to subsequent generations. They were childhood friends and studied with the same scholars.[10] Despite the disparity between the poor boy and the rich boy, and later between the man of misfortune and the man whose life was always

10. *Berakhot* 48a: "Abaye and Rava [when boys] were once sitting in the presence of Rabba. Said Rabba to them: 'To whom do we address the benedictions?' They

comfortable and complete, and despite their ongoing controversies over a myriad of issues, their close friendship lasted a lifetime.

Abaye and Rava, like the Study Houses which they headed, never dissented over personal matters, but always over basic principles; their disputes stemmed from profound personal and philosophical differences. Abaye, the "unfortunate and wise" man[11] whose rulings were generally not accepted as halakha, is nevertheless a formidable participant in the halakhic dialectic throughout the generations and stands, alongside Rava, as one of the two pillars upon which the Talmud rests.

replied: 'To the All-Merciful.' 'And where does the All-Merciful abide?' Rava pointed to the roof; Abaye went outside and pointed to the sky. Said Rabba to them: 'Both of you will become Rabbis.'"

11. See Ecclesiastes 4:13.

Chapter thirteen

Rav Ashi

Rav Ashi, the head of the yeshiva at Sura, is considered the editor, or rather the principal architect, of the Babylonian Talmud. The Talmud itself, which was sealed only after Rav Ashi's death, regards him as one of the three figures in Jewish history who combined both Torah learning and worldly greatness, and who were the sole leaders of the Jewish people in their respective periods.[1]

Torah and worldly matters were generally mutually exclusive realms in Judaism – not for political reasons, but as a function of the characters and abilities of the personalities involved. Nevertheless, throughout the generations there always existed the aspiration that Torah and worldly concerns be integrated in one person, that those who master mundane affairs should also have mastery of Torah and vice versa. Such a synthesis, however, only seldom occurred, so that alongside – sometimes in opposition to – the lay leaders of the Jewish people were its spiritual leaders, who often had no political significance whatsoever.

1. *Gittin* 59a: "Between Moshe and Rebbi we do not find one who was supreme both in Torah and in worldly affairs… between Rebbi and Rav Ashi there was no one who was supreme both in Torah and in worldly affairs."

It is therefore quite amazing that so very little is known about Rav Ashi, a figure who filled such a central historic role. We know nothing of his family origins, not even his father's name (although it may be assumed that the great wealth which sustained him was family heritage), nor do we know who Rav Ashi's teachers were. While we find him in discussions with scholars of the preceding generation, he never figures in them as a pupil before his teachers. He appears instead a disciple-colleague, that is, with a standing of his own – even when he was very young, less than twenty years old. Rav Ashi's position in the scholarly community was so extraordinary, that an eminent sage such as Ravina (the First), a prominent sage and considerably older than Rav Ashi, considered himself Rav Ashi's disciple-colleague.[2]

Rav Ashi could not have been much older than twenty when he attained full stature as head of the Sura yeshiva, a position he held for some sixty years.[3] This fact is quite surprising since leadership of the great yeshivot of Sura and Pumbedita was then a most distinguished and influential role, both locally and for all Jewry. When the Geonim wanted to say that someone became head of a yeshiva, they used the phrase, "Rabbi so-and-so reigned," likening his status to that of a king.

In Rav Ashi's time, the yeshiva at Pumbedita was destroyed, or at least ceased to function. The Jewish community in the Land of Israel – suffering greatly from the persecutions of the Byzantine Emperors who strove to convert the Jews to Christianity – no longer carried great spiritual weight. Thus, the head of the Sura yeshiva was not just first among equals in Babylonia, but the foremost Jewish leader of the period. In the political realm, too, Rav Ashi was considered the uncontested de facto leader of the entire Jewish world, whose authority was accepted even by the exilarch (even though he had no blood ties to him).

Rav Ashi left behind more than a monument. He bequeathed his entire spiritual being within the magnum opus of the Babylonian Tal-

2. *Eruvin* 63a: "Ravina examined the slaughterer's knife in [the town of] Babylon. Said Rav Ashi to him, 'Why does the Master act in this manner?' The other replied '... and I too am the Master's colleague as well as disciple.'"
3. This, according to Geonic traditions, which are considered reliable and accurate, having been based upon notes and written material of the yeshivot themselves.

mud – not just in the halakhic rulings that he himself established, but also in all of the Talmudic discussions and dicta in which he is not even mentioned. The entire Babylonian Talmud is, in away, a reflection of Rav Ashi's figure, mode of thought, and creativity; after all, everything in the Talmud is the outcome of the unique pattern that he molded.

We know too little about the redaction of the Talmud to establish whether it was done orally or in writing. Given the method of Torah study in those generations, the editing could indeed have been done orally, and in this sense, the Babylonian Talmud is a distillation, a sort of hologram of Torah study as it was conducted in Rav Ashi's yeshiva and of contemporary life and events.

Over the sixty years in which Rav Ashi served as the head of the Sura yeshiva, he taught one tractate of the Mishna at each one of the *Yarḥei Kalla,* along with its traditional commentaries as they had been orally transmitted over the generations. Unlike other scholars, however, Rav Ashi worked systematically: each semester, a different one of the sixty Mishna Tractates was studied, so that over a span of thirty years, he covered the entire Talmud. This review of all the tractates was actually a first redaction of the Babylonian Talmud. In the Talmud it is referred to as the "*mahadura kamma,*" the "first review." The second review, "*mahadura batra,*" is Rav Ashi's second overview of the Talmud, done in the course of his second thirty years as head of the yeshiva. The differences between the two versions are recorded in various places in the Talmud.[4] These two successive editions molded a particular style of study, whether written or oral, and created the basic pattern of the Talmud.

Thus, we owe the creation of the Babylonian Talmud to the integration of Torah and worldly greatness, combined with the longevity with which Rav Ashi was blessed, and which enabled him to consolidate and conclude the enterprise begun in his youth.

The redaction of the Talmud was an enormously complex undertaking due, inter alia, to its unique structure. Although all Talmudic

4. *Bava Batra* 157b: "Ravina said: 'In the first version, Rav Ashi told us [that] the first [creditor] acquired [the right over the land]; the second version of Rav Ashi [however], told us [that the land was] to be divided. And the law is [that the land] is to be divided.'" See Rashi who quotes from the Responsa of Rav Ḥai Gaon.

sugyot start out in the Mishna, they then branch out – not in a particularly logical order, but in a continuous associative stream, one topic leading to another. In terms of structure – although certainly not in essence or content – the Talmud somewhat resembles stream of consciousness novels. An initial topic often contains another issue that requires clarification, and in the course of discussion it turns out that that second point, too, needs to be elucidated. Thus the Talmud proceeds, sailing from one topic to another, sometimes in minor digressions of a line or two, sometimes in lengthy diversions which extend over several pages of text. Certain halakhot can therefore be found in tractates whose central issue is totally unrelated. The laws pertaining to mourning, for example, are found in the Tractate of *Mo'ed Katan*; the laws of Ḥanukka appear in the Tractate of *Shabbat*; and the laws of tefillin appear in the Tractate of *Menahot*.[5] These combinations are not coincidental; the issues are indeed related, but the links are associative and not logical.

The unique essence of the Talmud is further accentuated when compared with another text that is also a summary of the halakha: Maimonides' legal code, *Yad HaḤazaka*. Maimonides' book is organized in coherent fashion; the topics and the laws appear in logical order, in the appropriate sections, whereas in the Talmud, topics seem to be found everywhere and in every form. This, however, is not a matter of coincidence or sloppy editing, but the consequence of Rav Ashi's overall conception of the manner in which the Oral Law should be transmitted to the coming generations.

Although the ostensible aim of the Talmud is to synopsize the halakhot of the Oral Law, halakhic decision is most definitely not its sole purpose. Alongside the halakhic opinions that were accepted in practice, the Talmud records dissenting opinions as well. The Talmud is not an outline drawn up by an individual in order to teach others or to transmit conclusions; it is the actual give-and-take itself, the live flow of the learning process. Rav Ashi wished to preserve not the

5. Tractate *Mo'ed Katan* deals with the intermediate days of the holidays; Tractate *Shabbat* deals with the laws of the Sabbath; and Tractate *Menaḥot* deals with Temple offerings.

halakhic decisions nor this or that Talmudic issue, but the very movement of the study process, and that, within the set context of a written book, which no longer develops or regenerates itself. He is not like an architect who builds a house; he is like an artist who strives to breathe life into an inanimate statue. Rav Ashi attempted to do the seemingly impossible: to retain mobility and flexibility, the unanswered question and the probing exploration, within a format which is written, edited, and concretely defined.

To prevent the Talmud from becoming a random collection of discourses, Rav Ashi adopted two principles simultaneously. First, he formulated and encapsulated the history of ideas, the progression of the most significant discussions which took place in the three hundred years or more before his time. Thus he summarized not just current solutions for contemporary problems, but the major issues that had engaged the minds of the scholars throughout those generations. More than once he created entire constructs of postulations that do not arrive at any final conclusion. For him, it was not the "bottom line" that mattered but the process – the question, and on occasion even the error. It was critical to demonstrate how decisions were derived, and what obstacles and problems were overcome along the way.

Rav Ashi's second principle was to organize the material as precisely as possible. And indeed, despite the associative flow from subject to subject, each individual sentence is very accurately edited in terms of word order, sentence order, the syntactic position of proper names, nuances, etc. For instance: "Rabbi so-and-so said" means something different from "said Rabbi so-and-so"; questions that come in a sequence are always consecutive, not random; when two halakhic opinions are brought, the second one is always halakhically binding; and so on. All these, and many other elements, are the basis for future determination of the halakha.

The twofold difficulty in editing the Talmud lay, then, in preserving mobility and flexibility within a fixed entity while maintaining precision. Rav Ashi had to ensure that those seemingly inconclusive discussions and questions and answers would serve as well-defined and exceedingly accurate material, from which it would be possible to draw practical conclusions in the future. What may, at first glance, appear as haphazard Talmudic redaction is, in fact, the result of great meticulousness which succeeded in retaining the sense of freedom while presenting exactly what the sages wished to express.

Appendices

Glossary

Aggada: A genre that includes a variety of stories and comments about Biblical heroes and other Jewish historical figures, parables, aphorisms, and homilies, which are found in the Talmud and in the Midrash.

Amora (pl. amoraim): Talmudic sage from after the tannaitic period until the final redaction of the Talmud (220–500 C.E.). The amoraim interpreted the statements of the tannaim and expanded upon them.

Av Beit Din: The greatest man in the *Sanhedrin,* second only to the *Nasi*; head of the *beit din*.

Avot deRabbi Natan: A small tractate of the Talmud, a kind of *tosefta* or *baraita* to *Pirkei Avot,* attributed to Rabbi Natan the Babylonian.

Bar Kokhba: Shimon bar Kokhba (known also as Bar Koziva), leader of the *Great Revolt*. Rabbi Akiva, and many others, thought he was the Messiah.

Baraita (pl. *Baraitot*): Compilations of halakha which were not included in the Mishna.

Beit Din: Rabbinical court.

Beit Hillel: The students and the students-of-the-students of Hillel the Elder (see Chapter 1). They lived in the last generations of the Second Temple Era and the first generations after the destruction and generally tended to a more lenient approach to halakha.

Beit Midrash (pl. *batei midrash*): A house for the study of the Mishna and the Talmud, as well as for prayer (see also *Yeshiva*).

Beit Shammai: The students and the students-of-the-students of Shammai the Elder (see Chapter 2). They lived in the last generations of the Second Temple Era and the first generations after the destruction and generally tended to a more strict interpretation of halakha.

Kohen: A priest who performs the holy tasks of the Temple worship; a descendant of Aaron.

Exilarch: The leader of the Jewish communities in Babylon (parallel to the title of *Nasi* in the Land of Israel). All the exilarchs traced their descent from the House of David.

Gaon (pl. Geonim): See: Geonic Period.

Geonic Period: 589–1038 C.E., over 450 years in which the Geonim, the heads of the Babylonian yeshivot in Sura and Pumbedita, served as the supreme halakhic authority in the Jewish world.

Great Revolt: A Jewish revolt against the Roman conquest led by Bar Kochba. The revolt took place between 132–135 C.E., some sixty years after the destruction of the Second Temple. It started out auspiciously and aroused great Messianic hopes. It ended, however, with the fall of the city of Beitar and devastating destruction: over 500,000 Jews died, many others were sold in slavery, and the land of Judea was practically laid waste. In addition, the Romans enacted severe antireligious decrees and executed the Ten Martyrs.

Halakha: The legal part of the Torah (both the Written and the Oral) which defines actual practice. Its origins are Divine. Its principles are written in the Five Books of Moses and greatly expanded in the Mishna, the Talmud, and later codes.

Halakhic: Pertaining to halakha.

Halakhot: Specific halakhic rulings.

Ḥanukka: An eight-day festival of candle-lighting, starting on the 25th of the month of Kislev. This festival celebrates the purification of the Temple in Jerusalem and the resumption of Temple worship in the Hasmonean period (2nd to 1st century B.C.E.).

Havayot deRav uShmuel; *Havayot deAbaye veRava*: Investigative discussions and arguments between sages that form the basis for Talmudic discussion and study throughout the ages. The most famous are the discussions between Rav and Shmuel (see Chapters 8–9) and those between Abaye (see Chapter 12) and Rava.

Herod: King of Judea between 37 and 4 B.C.E. Of Edomite origin, he entered into the dynasty of Hasmonean Kings by marrying Miriam the Hasmonean (whom he eventually executed) and ruled thanks to Roman support. Herod was a Hellenistic-style despot, deeply despised and hated by the Jewish leadership and masses throughout his reign. He severely weakened all the autonomous Jewish institutions and abolished, de facto, the rule of Torah. As a gesture of loyalty to Judaism, he undertook the gigantic project of renovating the Temple in Jerusalem, making it the most beautiful edifice of the period.

Lulav: A palm leaf before it is fully developed and opened. It is one of the four species which Jews are commanded to take during the Festival of Sukkot. The other three are the myrtle, willow branch, and etrog – a species of citrus fruit.)

Megillat Ta'anit: An ancient book, part of which was composed before the destruction of the Second Temple. It includes a list of thirty-five days commemorated as festivals, in which it was forbidden to fast. Its rulings were in force until the third century C.E., when it was annulled by the sages.

Middot (*principles*): The summary of the principles and methods of exegesis and determining halakhic rulings from the Written Torah, as set by Hillel the Elder and subsequently by Rabbi Yishmael. See Chapter 1.

Midrash: An exegetic part of the Oral Law which explains the Written Torah by way of parable, *Aggada,* and homilies; a term which includes various collections of homilies, etc., of our sages.

Midrash Aggada: *Aggadic* exegesis; ancient collections of *aggada.* The main ones are *Midrash Rabba* (on the Five Books of Moses and the Five Scrolls) and *Midrash Tanḥuma.*

Midrash Halakha: Halakhic exegesis; ancient books of Jewish Oral Law which deal with halakha. The most important are *Mekhilta* (on Exodus), *Sifra* (on Leviticus), and *Sifrei* (on Numbers and Deuteronomy).

Mishna: The first and most fundamental collection of halakha of the Oral Torah. Its contents were transmitted orally for many generations until they were committed to writing by Rebbi (see Chapter 7). The Mishna is divided into six volumes (*sedarim*), each volume (*seder*) is divided into tractates, each tractate into chapters, and each chapter into mishnayot (singular – mishna). The six *sedarim* are: *Zera'im* (agricultural laws), *Mo'ed* (holy days), *Nashim* (family laws), *Nezikin* (civil law), *Kodashim* (Temple related), *Taharot* (ritual purity).

Mishnaic Period: Fourth century B.C.E. to ca. 200 C.E., the period in which the collections of halakhot that served as the basis for the Mishna were formed, and the Mishna was compiled.

mitzva (pl. mitzvot): Divine commandments as they are to be found in the Written and Oral Torah and in the writings of our sages.

Nasi (pl. *Nesi'im*): The leader of the *Sanhedrin* (see also *Av Beit Din*). There was no clear-cut division of function between the two heads of the *Sanhedrin*, except that the *Nasi* sometimes also wielded political power.

Pairs: The five pairs of Jewish sages during the Second Temple period, in the period between the Great Assembly and the first of the tannaim (see *Pirkei Avot* 1:1–15). One of them was *Nasi* and the other *Av Beit Din*. The pairs were: Yossi ben Yo'ezer and Yossi ben Yoḥanan; Yehoshua ben Peraḥya and Nitai HaArbeli; Yehuda ben Tabbai and Shimon ben Shettaḥ; Shemaya and Avtalyon; Hillel and Shammai.

Perushim (*Pharisees*): The main sect of sages and Torah scholars who studied and expanded the Oral Torah.

Peshat: The simplest, most literal, and "common sense" meaning of the Torah and the Talmud.

Pilpul: In its positive sense, the term refers to the most profound and exhaustive kind of discussion, which deals with every possible aspect of the issue at hand; it is compared to a brave fighter who waves his sword deftly in every possible direction. In the negative sense, it refers to the kind of Talmudic discussion that developed in the course of time, which involved excessive hair-splitting and overanalysis of issues, taking them out of context and thus distorting them.

Pirkei Avot: A tractate of the Mishna that contains aphorisms and practical and moral guidance from our sages.

Principles: See *Middot.*

Rashi: Rabbi Shlomo Yitzḥaki (Trois, France, 1040–1105), the greatest Talmud commentator of all generations and among the most important Biblical commentators.

Rosh HaShana: The Jewish New Year, a festival which takes place on the first and second days of the month of Tishrei. It is considered the day of judgment for the entire universe. The shofar is blown.

Sanhedrin: The council of elders and the supreme Jewish court of seventy-one judges in the Land of Israel, which first convened at the Temple.

Semikha: Literally, "Laying of Hands": (1) to transfer the authority for making halakhic rulings and for judging from one sage to another; (2) the person who brings a sacrifice lays his hands on the head of the designated animal, prior to sacrifice, to confess his sins, etc. The two "layings of hands" are similar: a person thereby transfers his intention to the person/animal upon whom the hands are placed.

Shabbat boundaries: A radius of 2000 cubits outside a settled area in which one is allowed to walk on Shabbat.

Shekhina: One of the names for the Divine Presence in this world.

Shema: Three short Torah portions (Deuteronomy 6:4–9 and 11:13–21, and Numbers 15:37–41) which are recited every morning and evening and before going to sleep.

Shofar: A wind instrument made of ram's horn, now blown only on Rosh HaShana and Yom Kippur, but used in ancient times for convening the army and declaring festivals.

Sifra: See *Midrash Halakha.*

Sifrei: See *Midrash Halakha.*

Sukka (*Tabernacle*): A temporary structure made of wooden planks, branches, palm leaves, etc., in which Jews are commanded to live during the seven-day festival of Sukkot.

Sukkot: A festival celebrated from the 15th to the 21st of the month of Tishrei, by living in the Sukka, taking the four species (see lulav), and rejoicing.

Sugya (pl. *sugyot*): A wide-ranging treatment of a particular topic by way of halakhic dialectical investigation of its tannaitic sources. These oral investigations were later edited and recorded and constitute the basic literary units of the Talmud.

Tallit: A four-cornered garment, now worn during prayer and at the time of the Mishna and the Talmud worn all day long. The Torah commands Jews to put tzitzit, a special fringe, on each one of the four corners of the garment, as a reminder to perform all of God's commandments.

Talmud: The most important book in the history and culture of the Jewish people, the Talmud includes the Mishna. It was created over the course of some 1,000 years, both in the Land of Israel and in Babylon. There are, in fact, two Talmuds:

The Babylonian Talmud was compiled in various Yeshivot by amoraim from Babylon and from the Land of Israel. It was edited by Rav Ashi (see Chapter 13) and finalized in the following generation, in the beginning of the 6th century C.E., by Rav Yossi. It contains 37 Tractates, in the order of the six *Sedarim* (see Mishna) as follows: From *Zera'im*, only to Tractate *Berakhot;* all of *Mo'ed, Nashim, Nezikin,* and *Kodashim,* and from *Taharot* only to Tractate *Nidda*. It is written in a mixture of Hebrew and Babylonian Aramaic and has been most widely studied by Jews all over the world and throughout all generations. Numerous commentaries on it have been written, most notably those of Rashi and the *Tosafot.*

The Jerusalem Talmud was composed by amoraim in the Land of Israel, especially in the cities of Tiberias, Zippori, and Caesarea, as well as by some Babylonian amoraim. It was edited mainly by Rabbi Yoḥanan (see chapter 10) and finalized some 150 years before the Babylonian Talmud. It includes four full tractates: *Zera'im, Mo'ed, Nashim,* and *Nezikin,* and a part of Tractate *Nidda*. It is written in the Israeli-Aramaic dialect and has been studied and expounded much less than the Babylonian Talmud.

Tanḥuma: See *Midrash Aggada*.

Tanna (pl. tannaim): A sage during and after the Second Temple period, from Shimon HaTzadik (the end of the 3rd century B.C.E.) until the students of Rebbi, in the beginning of the 3rd century C.E. (see chapter 7). The Tannaim created the Mishna, the *Tosefta,* the *Midrash,* and more.

Tefillin (*phylacteries*): The Torah (Deuteronomy 6:8) commands men to tie tefillin on their arm and head each day. They consist of cube-shaped leather boxes containing parchment on which four passages from the Torah (Deuteronomy 6:4–9; 11:13–21; Exodus 13:1–10; 13:11–16) are written. The boxes are each attached to long black leather straps used to tie them to the head and the arm. Tefillin are holy and should not be worn in an unclean place or at a time when a person cannot maintain his body in a state of cleanliness. In ancient times, tefillin were worn the entire day; now, however, it is customary to wear them only during the morning prayer. Tefillin are not worn on Shabbat and festivals.

Ten Martyrs: Ten great Jewish personalities of the Tannaitic Period executed (sometimes very cruelly) by the Romans for continuing to teach Torah in spite of Roman anti-religious decrees. They were: Rabbi Akiva, Rabbi Ḥanina ben Tradion, Rabbi Yishmael the High Priest, Rabbi Yehuda ben Bava, Rabbi Ḥutzpit the Interpreter, Rabban Shimon ben Gamliel, Rabbi Elazar ben Shamua, Rabbi Ḥanina ben Ḥakhinai, Rabbi Yeshevav the Scribe, Rabbi Yehuda ben Damma.

Tosafot: Commentaries, criticism, and new interpretations to the Talmud which were added by Rashi's grandchildren and other contemporary Rabbis to Rashi's commentary on the Babylonian Talmud.

Tosefta: The collection of halakha which was compiled by the last tannaim, Rabbi Ḥiyya and Rabbi Oshaya, as additions to the Mishna.

Tzedukim (*Sadducees*): A sect that existed in Judea during the Second Temple era, which denied the validity of the Oral Torah and was therefore always in confrontation with the Perushim.

Tzitzit: The Torah commands (Numbers 15:37–41) men to place fringes on the four corners of garments with four or more corners. The fringes are made up of four threads, generally of wool, which are folded over to make up eight. The upper part of the tzitzit is knotted in a prescribed manner, and from it hang the eight half-threads. Originally, three of the four threads were white, and the fourth was dyed blue. The obligation of tzitzit applies only during the daytime (see tallit).

Yad HaḤazaka: A monumental work by Maimonides, unique in the history of Jewish religious literature subsequent to the Mishna, in which the entire contents of the Oral Torah is summarized in perfect logical order, in a lucid, authoritative, and unequivocal style and in beautiful Hebrew prose.

Yarḥei Kalla: The months of Adar (at the end of winter) and Elul (at the end of summer) in which Torah scholars in Babylonia would convene in the yeshivot in order to study Torah.

Yeshiva (pl. yeshivot): A house for the study of Mishna and Talmud (See also *beit midrash*).

Yom Kippur: The Day of Atonement, the 10th day of the month of Tishrei. A day of fasting and prayer, considered the holiest day of the year.

Annotated Bibliography

Arukh: A comprehensive alphabetical lexicon for the Talmud and the Midrash, containing dictionary definitions and extensive explanations, sources, and commentaries, mainly from the Geonic period. Was written by Rabbi Natan ben Yeḥiel of Rome (ca. 1035–1106). Has been widely used throughout the ages by Jewish scholars the world over.

Avot deRabbi Natan: See Glossary.

Babylonian Talmud: See Glossary.

Jerusalem Talmud: See Glossary.

Maimonides: Commentary to the Mishna: One of the most important commentaries on the Mishna, written by Rabbi Moshe ben Maimon (Maimonides), the greatest Jewish Medieval sage (1138–1204). Written originally in Arabic, between 1161–1168.

Maimonides: *Yad HaḤazaka*: See Glossary.

Megillat Ta'anit: See Glossary.

Midrash Raba (on the Pentateuch and the five Scrolls): A collection of *Midrashei Aggada* which were edited in various periods and put together as one book by the printers. Over time, it became immensely popular among scholars as well as the simple folk. A number of important commentaries were written on it.

Midrash Shoḥer Tov: *Midrash Aggada* on Psalms. The date and place of composition are unknown.

Midrash Tanḥuma (Buber edition): *Midrash Aggada* on the Pentateuch, attributed to Rabbi Tanḥuma bar Abba and probably composed in the Land of Israel towards the end of the fourth century C.E. It is based on the three-year cycle of Torah reading. Its basic structure is that of a halakhic question, followed by an answer and an extended homily with parables and stories.

Pesikta deRav Kahana: An ancient *Midrash Aggada* on some of the Torah portions and the Haftarot (portions from the Prophets that follow the Torah reading), probably composed in the Land of Israel around the 5th century C.E. It contains homilies for the Shabbat of Ḥanukka, Pesaḥ, Shavuot, Rosh HaShana, Yom Kippur, Sukkot, and others.

Pirkei Avot: See Glossary.

Pirkei deRabbi Eliezer: A *Midrash Aggada* from the 8th century, of which we have only the first 54 chapters. It begins with the personal history of Rabbi Eliezer the Great (see chapter 5) and then gives a chronological description of events from Creation to the Israelite wanderings in the desert. It was obviously written by one person and most probably drew not only from the Bible but also from the Apocrypha, the apocalyptic literature of the Second Temple period, and Arabic folk tales of the Ummayah dynasty period.

Rabbi Ovadia of Bertinoro (erroneously named "Bartenura"): An Italian-born rabbi and Jewish leader who emigrated to the Land of Israel, was the leader of the Jewish community of Jerusalem, and died in Jerusalem c. 1516. He is famous mainly for his simple and clear commentary on the Mishna, which has been widely studied, and has had two important commentaries written on it.

Rashbam (on Pesaḥim): Commentary of Rashbam to Tractate *Pesaḥim*. Rashbam, an abbreviation for Rabbi Shmuel ben Meir, was Rashi's grandson and student (France, 1080–1160), and one of the greatest *Tosafists* (see Glossary: *Tosafot*) and Biblical commentators. His commentary is characterized by strict literal interpretation.

Rashi's commentary to the Babylonian Talmud: The most important commentary on the Talmud, written by Rabbi Shlomo Yitzḥaki (Rashi); see Glossary.

Sifra and *Sifrei*: *Midrash Halakha* for the books of Leviticus (*Sifra*), and Numbers and Deuteronomy (*Sifrei*). They are, in fact, collections of *baraitot* compiled and edited by various editors in the Land of Israel, around the end of the fourth century C.E. These commentaries refer, in order, to each chapter and verse, and sometimes to each word, in the respective books. See Glossary.

Tanna d'Vei Eliyahu: Also known as *Seder Eliyahu*. It is a unique *Midrash Aggada*, written in very personal and poetic language. The format is the tales of a traveling sage. The book has an ethical-didactic bent and deals mainly with the Torah commandments and the reasons for them, Torah study, prayer, and other religious-ethical values, as reflected in the stories of the Patriarchs. The book is divided in two parts: *Seder Eliyahu Raba* and *Seder Eliyahu Zuta*. The time and place of composition are unknown.

Teshuvot HaGeonim, Sha'arei Teshuva: During the Geonic Period, a vast literary body of questions-and-answers was composed as a result of intense correspondence between the heads of the Babylonian Yeshivot of Sura and Pumbedita and Jews from all over the Diaspora. This book is one of many to have been published. A large portion of this literature is still in manuscripts.

Tosefta: See Glossary.

A Historical Framework

PRE-TANNAITIC AND TANNAITIC PERIOD

Dates	Name and Generation	Historical Events in the Land of Israel	World Events
4th Century B.C.E. 3rd Century B.C.E.	 Shimon haTzaddik Antigonus of Sokho	The conquest of the Land of Israel by Alexander the Great	Greek rule in the East
2nd Century B.C.E.	Yossi ben Yo'ezer Yossi ben Yoḥanan Yehoshua ben Peraḥya Nitai haArbeli	Hasmonean Period	Decline of the Seleucid power
1st Century B.C.E.	Yehuda ben Tabbai Shimon ben Shettaḥ Shemaya, Avtalyon	Alexander Yannai	

Dates	Name and Generation	Historical Events in the Land of Israel	World Events
30 B.C.E.–20 C.E.	**Hillel** **Shammai** 1. Gamliel I HaZaken	Herodian Period	Rise of the Roman Empire in the East; Augustus
40 C.E.–80 C.E. 80 C.E.–110 C.E.	2. Shimon ben Gamliel I **Yoḥanan ben Zakkai** 3. **Eliezer ben Hyrcanus** **Yehoshua ben Ḥanania** **Elisha ben Avuya (Aḥer)**	Destruction of the Second Temple	Vespasian, Titus
110 C.E.–135 C.E. 135 C.E.–170 C.E.	4. Akiva 5. Shimon ben Gamliel II Shimon bar Yoḥai Meir	Bar Kokhba Revolt	Hadrian
170 C.E.–200 C.E.	6. **Yehuda HaNasi (Rebbi)**	Final redaction of the Mishna	Caracalla, Alexander Severus

THE AMORAIC PERIOD

Dates	**Name and Generation**		**World Events**
	The Land of Israel	*Babylonia*	
Transitional Period 200 C.E.–220 C.E.	Oshaya Rabba Bar Kappara Ḥiyya		
220 C.E.–250 C.E.	1. Ḥanina bar Ḥama Yannai Yehoshua ben Levi	**Rav** **Shmuel**	The Sassanid kingdom in Babylonia
250 C.E.–290 C.E.	2. **Yoḥanan** **Resh Lakish**	Huna Yehuda ben Yehezkel	
290 C.E.–320 C.E.	3. Ammi, Assi, Zera	Rabba bar Naḥmani Yosef bar Ḥiyya	
320 C.E.–350 C.E.	4. Hillel II, Yonah, Yossi bar Zevida	**Abaye**, Rava, Rami bar Ḥama	Christianity becomes an officially recognized religion in the Roman Empire
350 C.E.–375 C.E.	5. Mana II, Tanḥuma bar Abba	Pappa	
375 C.E.–425 C.E.	6	**Ashi**, Ravina I	Final redaction of the Talmud
425 C.E.–460 C.E.	7	Mar bar Rav Ashi	Roman Empire divided into East and West

Dates	Name and Generation		World Events
	The Land of Israel	*Babylonia*	
460 C.E.–500 C.E.	8	Rabbah Tosafaah Ravina II	Fall of the Roman Empire in the West Final redaction of the Babylonian Talmud

Index

Z

About the Author

Rabbi Adin Steinsaltz (Even-Israel) is a teacher, philosopher, social critic and prolific author who has been hailed by *Time* magazine as a "once-in-a-millennium scholar." His lifelong work in Jewish education earned him the Israel Prize, his country's highest honor.

Born in Jerusalem in 1937 to secular parents, Rabbi Steinsaltz studied physics and chemistry at the Hebrew University. He established several experimental schools and, at the age of 24, became Israel's youngest school principal.

In 1965, he began his monumental Hebrew translation and commentary on the Talmud. To date, he has published 38 of the anticipated 46 volumes. The Rabbi's classic work of Kabbalah, The Thirteen Petalled Rose, was first published in 1980 and now appears in eight languages. In all, Rabbi Steinsaltz has authored some 60 books and hundreds of articles on subjects ranging from zoology to theology to social commentary.

Continuing his work as a teacher and spiritual mentor, Rabbi Steinsaltz established a network of schools and educational institutions in Israel and the former Soviet Union. He has served as scholar in residence at the Woodrow Wilson Center for International Studies in Washington, D.C. and the Institute for Advanced Studies at Princeton

University. His honorary degrees include doctorates from Yeshiva University, Ben Gurion University of the Negev, Bar Ilan University, Brandeis University, and Florida International University.

Rabbi Steinsaltz lives in Jerusalem. He and his wife have three children and ten grandchildren.

The fonts used in this book are from the Arno family

Other works by Adin Steinsaltz
available from Maggid

A Dear Son to Me

Biblical Images

The Candle of God

The Essential Talmud

The Tales of Rabbi Nachman of Bratslav

Teshuvah

The Thirteen Petalled Rose

Maggid Books
The best of contemporary Jewish thought from
Koren Publishers Jerusalem Ltd.